Psychic Sex

Beckah Boyd

International Psychic Medium

4880 Lower Valley Road, Atglen, Pennsylvania 19310

Disclaimer: The purpose of this book is to educate. It is not intended to give medical or psychological therapy and is no replacement for that. Whenever there is concern for physical or mental illness, a professional should be sought. The sexual positions, ideas, and rituals found within this text are not meant for everyone. The author and publisher shall have neither liability nor responsibility to any person or entity with respect to any loss, damage, injury, or ailment caused or alleged to be caused directly or indirectly by the information or lack of information within this book.

Images unless otherwise noted in the text are by the author. Stock photos have been used in this book by the author. Some photos are Courtesy of www.bigstockphoto.com. Labradorite Beads On String 2 © Heather Weaver. Singing bowls © Erik de Graaf. Girl © Bruce Rolff; Aspnaked Hip © Gustavo Alfredo Schaufelberger Pirron; Bod G1 © 1911; Girl in water © Yuri Arcurs; Egypt tomb art©William McCarthy; Abu Simbel heads, Egypt, Africa © CJ Photo; Notre Dam Cathedral Rene DROUYER; Victorian couple © Sahuad; High Society © Dmitry Tereshchenko; Brain (Balls of Energy) © ktsdesign; Lightning bolt © William McCarthy; Drawing © Orlando Rosu; Nuances of the Flesh © Les Byerley; Nude Adult Woman © Sean Nel; White satin or silk © Marilyn Volan; Passionate couple © Andriy Bezuglov; Tenderness © Denis Raev; Kissing in bed © Lev Dolgachov; A Happy Couple © Mehmet Alci; Pregnant Lady © Mehmet Alci; Couple in Love © Mehmet Alci; Love on the Beach © Andreas Gradin; Romantic and cute ©Yuri Arcurs, Lightening © bram janssens, Aphrodite © Dwight Smith. Water leaves and ripples © ifong, Rose bouquet © wpcasey.

Copyright © 2010 Beckah Boyd

Library of Congress Control Number: 2010937138

All rights reserved. No part of this work may be reproduced or used in any form or by any means—graphic, electronic, or mechanical, including photocopying or information storage and retrieval systems—without written permission from the publisher.

The scanning, uploading and distribution of this book or any part thereof via the Internet or via any other means without the permission of the publisher is illegal and punishable by law. Please purchase only authorized editions and do not participate in or encourage the electronic piracy of copyrighted materials.

"Schiffer," "Schiffer Publishing Ltd. & Design," and the "Design of pen and ink well" are registered trademarks of Schiffer Publishing Ltd.

Designed by Stephanie Daugherty
Type set in UnivrstyRoman Bd BT /New Baskerville BT

ISBN: 978-0-7643-3582-2
Printed in China

Schiffer Books are available at special discounts for bulk purchases for sales promotions or premiums. Special editions, including personalized covers, corporate imprints, and excerpts can be created in large quantities for special needs. For more information contact the publisher:

Dedication

To my clients, my friends, and my family. Thank you.

Schiffer Publishing Ltd.
4880 Lower Valley Road
Atglen, PA 19310
Phone: (610) 593-1777
Fax: (610) 593-2002
E-mail: Info@schifferbooks.com

For the largest selection of fine reference books on this and related subjects, please visit our web site at **www.schifferbooks.com**
We are always looking for people to write books on new and related subjects. If you have an idea for a book please contact us at the above address.

This book may be purchased from the publisher. Include $5.00 for shipping. Please try your bookstore first. You may write for a free catalog.

In Europe, Schiffer books are distributed by
Bushwood Books
6 Marksbury Ave.
Kew Gardens
Surrey TW9 4JF England
Phone: 44 (0) 20 8392-8585; Fax: 44 (0) 20 8392-9876
E-mail: info@bushwoodbooks.co.uk
Website: www.bushwoodbooks.co.uk

Acknowledgments

Thank you to the clients who opened up their homes and their marriages to me, to the Divine for leading me on this path. Thank you to Schiffer Publishing and especially Dinah Roseberry, my editor, for believing in my book ideas and never hesitating to pitch them. Thanks to Peter Schiffer, for going out on a limb! Thank you to Jess Digiacinto, my former editor at carrieanddanielle.com for giving me the inspiration to write the article *Success Through Orgasm* which ultimately led to this book. See girl! Dreams can happen!

Contents

Introduction   8

Sex in Our Culture   12

Who Are You in the Bedroom?   25

Creating a Complete   30
Psychic Sex Connection

Preparing Your Space   98
for the Psychic Sex Connection

How to Have A Psychic Sex Experience   117

The After-Sex Connection   142

Fertility   144

In Conclusion   156

Resources   158

Bibliography   160

Love's Philosophy

The fountains mingle with the river
And the rivers with the ocean,
The winds of Heaven mix forever
With a sweet emotion;
Nothing in the world is single;
All things by a law divine
In one spirit meet and mingle.
Why not I with thine?

~ Percy Bysshe Shelley

Body language like this shows a relationship pushing its limits.

Introduction

I grew up psychic; it was a family trait—all the women had it. Even some of the men did, although no one really acknowledged it for what it was. My mother was the first one to come out of the closet, so to speak. She trained me from a young age and let me know that my abilities were something to cherish, share, and be proud of. As I grew up, I learned that not everyone thought the way my mother did. As a psychic, I learned early on about relationships. My friend's parents would seem like the perfect couple but I always knew when there was trouble underneath the surface and what the cause was.

I saw families ripped apart by divorce, kids devastated by their parents' arguments and sometimes even physical fights. Then I saw the positive sides too, a couple who were completely compatible in every way. As I got older, and began seeing the energy between couples, I soon realized the differences. How, for some, the energy blended, and for others, their aura seemed to be in a constant state of defense or invasion of the others.

When I opened up my psychic consultations practice in the early 2000s, I discovered that most of the issues people were coming to see me about were their relationships, or lack thereof. I have had many couples come sit at my table looking for the answers to the rift in their relationships. I know it may sound as though they need a therapist more than a psychic, however, over the years working with energy and people in general I have come to realize two very important things. Firstly, the energy you emanate can tell you things before even you realize them; secondly, that energy also keeps a record of all of your past issues. Think of all the mental trauma and physical trauma you have gone through as scars on the body. Well, your energy will literally bear those scars.

If your energy and self is not completely whole, how can you believe that you can have a one hundred percent healthy relationship? You really cannot. However, people of the same ilk have a tendency to gravitate towards each other. This is not just a matter of fitting in. It is the Universe's way of showing you a mirror image, so that you can see what is wrong and needs to be fixed. In that same vein, when two people get together as a couple who have similar traumas in their past, that does not mean their relationship is doomed. On the contrary, it actually gives them the ability to grow together, learn from each other and evolve.

Nevertheless, this only works if they are open to the learning. Some people like the drama, like the excitement and energy that comes around when friends or lovers are having issues. If there are no issues, they will create more. I am the eternal optimist though, and when personalities like these come to my table with their partners, I find that pointing out their patterns with an objective eye really helps give clarity to the situation. This book is about healing and creating a healthy relationship, and sex, although not the key, is the greatest connector in a relationship. It has the power to heal, to touch the Universe, to manifest wants, and to create a psychic connection.

I first realized the impact of sex in my own relationship. It is the best stress reliever, the best pain medication, and the best comfort. At the same time, it can also be the biggest frustration, the greatest source of anger and humiliation. When sex is approached properly, it can create the ultimate connection between two people, one where you feel not only your own pleasure, but your partners as well, where afterwards you just know what your partner is thinking and when you feel as if you are the other person as much as you are yourself.

That is the Psychic Sex Connection.

One of the many positive goals that you can gain through using this book is the strengthening of the psychic connection between you and your partner.

You will pick up on their emotions more easily and sense when there are issues around them (even at a distance)—it is an absolute trippy experience for those who have not had any experiences with psychic ability before. In addition, because you are working with energy, you will get more sensitive to the energies around you, not just the energies of people, but places and things as well.

The psychic connection between you both can be intensified and strengthened overtime using the techniques outlined in this book.

I wrote this book for everyone and anyone looking to increase their own sensuality, to explore their sexuality, and to increase their psychic sensitivities. Part of working on your psychic self is tapping into your essential self, that part of you that is your essence that will never change.

Oftentimes when we are in a relationship, we feel as though we lose a piece of ourselves, and honestly, in most unhealthy relationships, you do. With this book, it will teach you to keep a firm hold on your essential self, to glory in your differences, and to worship yourself as the Deity you are, both *in* and *out* of the bedroom. It is not always going to be easy, and whenever you travel the road of self-exploration and appreciation, there will be bumps and obstacles. Sometimes you will fall flat on your face, others you will feel like a million bucks; but in the end, there will be a satisfaction and connection with the Universe and your partner, as you have never had before.

Sex In Our Culture

> "Analyze any human emotion, no matter how far it may be removed from the sphere of sex, and you are sure to discover somewhere the primal impulse."
>
> ~ *Sigmund Freud*

There was a great article on modern sex research in The Scientist back in 1994. In it they talked about the meaning of sex to the average student and the stigma still attached to the research. I like the beginning portion of the article which told what sex really means and I wanted to share it with you:

If sexual activity is a prickly issue for discussion in society and our daily lives, it appears no less so as a research topic in some areas of the scientific and medical communities. The very definition of the word sex seems troublesomely elusive for many researchers when it comes to classifying their investigative efforts and obtaining the funding to support them.

"When I ask my students to define sex, or sexuality," says physiology and anatomy professor Robert Friar of Ferris State University in Big Rapids, Mich., "their response is usually 'male-female.'

"But I tell them they are wrong. That is gender, not sex." In his class, Friar describes sexuality as "a diffused sensuality that permeates our whole personality and everything that we do."

"Sex research covers everything from A– to Z–anthropology to zoology," says Howard Ruppell, executive director of the Society for the Scientific Study of Sex, headquartered in Mount Vernon, Iowa, and an adjunct professor of social work at the University of Iowa. A functional definition, according to him and Friar, would include not only behavioral studies (typically characterized as sex research), but also all research pertaining to the structure and function of the sexual and reproductive systems and related organs, as well as their effects on other organs and systems.

An antique tile mosaic in which a word appears (happenstance?).

"A diffused sensuality that permeates our whole personality and everything that we do."

Truer words have never been spoken. Every society has always had a sometimes morbid fascination with sex, whether they frowned upon it or encouraged it with numerous partners. Sexual history always fascinated me, and I have noticed while writing this book that our sexual appetites and roles deeply affected not only our personal lives but also our governments, money, and more! It is amazing how one thing, so essential to our survival received such degradation and vilification overtime, but still has so much power over us. Yet it does. I believe that to completely understand something we must look back at the past; then we can move forward into the future. Therefore, I would like to look back in history and show you just what I mean.

Looking Back

Early Mesopotamia

Sex was always important even in early Mesopotamia where we can find the earliest engraving of a sexual act on a clay tablet. In their society, men were expected to have multiple wives and women. However, if a woman was found with another man she would be tied to the bed and beaten. It was the duty of the King to sleep with Priestess' of Ishtar in order to ensure good rains and success throughout the year. Sex and sex magic have gone hand in hand with our species for centuries and the act of having a ruler sleep with an embodiment of a deity is not a new one. It was believed in some cultures that an act such as this would imbue the King with sacred powers. In this instance, it is the power to bring rains and keep the land fertile. The Mesopotamian culture is filled with exotic tales of deities who battle each other through love. Such as the story of Enkidu and Gilgamesh.

Erotic sculptures decorating the ancient Vishvanath Hindu Temple at Khajuraho Uttar Pradesh India, 11th Century AD.

Enkidu and Gilgamesh

Gilgamesh was the King of Uruk, and there was no finer place. The people of Uruk commended the King believing that he was the son of Deities. "Two-thirds of him was divine, one-third human." Being driven by this spiritual power, he continued to expand his city, building two temples and a great wall to protect his lands. He was a great lover of women and it is said that he would carry brides off on their wedding days. He was a fighting man, and would start wars, killing many of the city's sons in the process. This did not please the male villagers at all and they said, "Gilgamesh leaves no son to his father; his lust leaves no bride to her groom; yet he is the shepherd of the city, strong, handsome, and wise." The Deities heard this and were deeply disappointed. They went to Aruru who originally created Gilgamesh and asked her to create someone more powerful to keep the young King in line. So Aruru gathered some clay and began to mould Enkidu. When she was finished, Enkidu came to earth, he was like man in the beginning, his most prominent feature being his hairiness. He ran with the animals, destroyed hunters' traps and filled in their pits.

    One day, a hunter had come to check on his traps and found Enkidu by a watering hole. He was so fearful of this large man-beast, he ran back to his father for counsel. His father advised him to go to Uruk and talk to Gilgamesh, "Ask him to give you a temple courtesan, so that the wild man may be subdued by a woman's power. When next he comes down to drink at the watering place he will embrace her, and then the wild beasts will reject him." This is exactly what happened, for six days and seven nights Enkidu satisfied himself with the prostitute. After he was completely spent, he tried to approach his herd of animals but they rejected him. When he tried to run after them, he found his legs and knees to be weak. However, the experience opened his mind and it seemed he had gained human understanding. He went back to the courtesan for comfort. She spoke to him of Uruk and Gilgamesh; Enkidu, realized how lonely he was as she spoke. She taught him how to act like a civilized man and upon their travel to the holy city, they came upon a peddler also headed to Uruk. The peddler informed Enkidu of Gilgamesh's lustful ways, stating that there was to be a wedding and that Gilgamesh was planning on taking his "first rights" (the King's right to bed a wife prior to the husband doing so). Enkidu was appalled by what he heard and rushed to the city to stop Gilgamesh. There people commented on how much he looked like their king.

    A bridal bed was made and the bridegroom made ready for the wedding night. His pleasure was foiled when Gilgamesh appeared to take his rights. Enkidu met him there; they fought each other, building too near collapse they were both so aggressive.

Eventually, Gilgamesh accepted Enkidu as part of himself, and they became the best of friends. However, this story is just one of many where one enemy fights another using sex as a means of gaining power. This is an age-old story, and even though it was written thousands of years ago it is still applicable to our society.

Egypt

Next, let us travel to Egypt, a sensual and sexual society, they believed their Universe was created by the aftermath of one of their god's self-pleasuring sessions. The Egyptian culture did not shy away from sex actually; they celebrated it and saw it as a beautiful integral part of human nature. Love was seen as the epitome of human emotion and elemental power. In Egyptian poetry, the words do not rhyme and the language is rudimentary but the passion and longing can be felt in every word that is written.

> I wish I were her Nubian slave who guards her steps.
> Then I would be able to see the colour of all her limbs!
> I wish I were her laundryman, just for a single month.
> Then I would flourish by donning [her garment] and be close to her body.
> I would wash away the unguent from her clothes and wipe my body in her dress . . .
> I wish I were the signet ring which guards her finger, then I would see her desire every day.
>
> (IFAO 1266 + Cairo 25218, 18-21)

In this one you can easily see the intermingling of African societies with those of the Egyptians—as well as the desperation felt by the unrequited love of the writer. Many of the Egyptian poems do not contain the more basic nature like the writings of the mythological Gods. It seemed that even though the Egyptians loved sex, the basic writings of it were kept for these divine beings. Although drawings were another matter entirely.

> O my god, my lotus flower! . . .
> It is lovely to go out and . . .
> I love to go and bathe before you.
> I allow you to see my beauty
> in a dress of the finest linen,
> drenched with fragrant unguent.
> I go down into the water to be with you
> and come up to you again with a red fish,
> looking splendid on my fingers.
> I place it before you . . .
> Come! Look at me!
>
> (IFAO 1266 + Cairo 25218, 7-11)

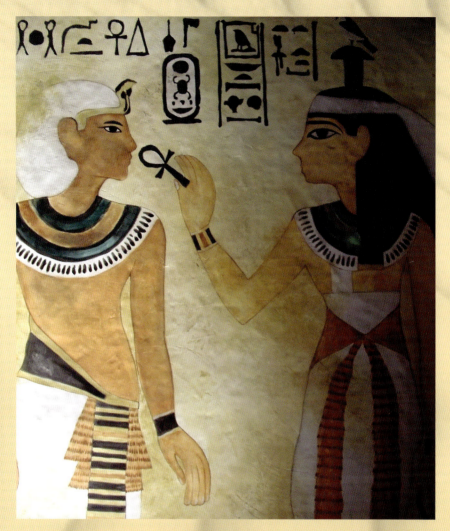

Symbolism runs rampant in this particular text. A red fish was an extremely erotic figure to the Egyptians as it represented the phallus. So a woman holding a big red fish...well, you get the idea. Egyptian men were so used to seeing half-naked women that they were completely desensitized to it. They focused primarily on what they couldn't see, and the challenge of overcoming the particular obstacle that the clothing represented by using their imagination. Much like men do today when they "look a woman up and down."

In comparison, the love between Gods was much more earthy and the language a lot more vivid. Such as in the creation story of Ra (seen here as Atem) and his two children:

Atem is he who masturbated in Iunu (On, Heliopolis). He took his phallus in his grasp that he might create orgasm by means of it, and so were born the twins Shu and Tefnut.

Homosexuality and incest were also present within Egyptian culture and their texts regarding their deities. In The Great Quarrel, Set (dark) and Horus (light) fight over the throne. Set tries to prove that Horus is illegitimate; when that does not work, he sets out to downright bully and humiliate his nephew:

Then Set said to Horus: "Come, let us have a feast day at my house." And Horus said to him: "I will, I will." Now when evening had come, a bed was prepared for them, and they lay down together. At night, Set let his member become stiff, and he inserted it between the thighs of Horus. And Horus placed his hand between his thighs and caught the semen of Set.

Horus then went to his mother and in disgust she cut off his hand and threw it in the marsh which allowed Horus' hand to regenerate. He then goes back to defeat Set.

The Egyptian way of life was rampant with free sexual love, couples, singles, they were very aware of the power of sex in birth, death, and rebirth. They believed that sex did exist in the afterlife and that they lived in representation of their earthy sensual gods and goddesses.

Greece and Rome

The Greeks and Romans were equally salacious societies. In Greece the philosopher and poet Anacreon often wrote about the love between two men. These meetings were not alluded to, but rather openly discussed. The elite male in Greek society was to be the mirror or representative of Zeus or Pan and the Satyrs they represented the animal aspect of sex. Romantic love was not common during this period and it seems in many of the eras following it. The man was expected to keep mistresses and multiple partners including males and they could often be found in the symposium rooms and party halls with the Hityrii, the servants of Aphrodite who were the most liberated women in their time, able to go where regular women dare not tread. These women were often cultured, educated, and sexually free to do as they pleased.

Looking at ancient Greece through Anacreon's eyes is quite an experience. It seems he was a bisexual male, who may have been a little promiscuous! Although he adored both the male and female anatomy like most men of his period, he was inherently skeptical when it came to the female mind and sexuality. Greek men believed that women were oversexed and insatiable.

Nowadays, we all know about sex toys, but where did they originate? Well, a few years ago, they found one that dated back 28,000 years. But it was used for phallus worship and as a flint stone. (Ouch.) In ancient Greece, however, they really loved their dildos. They would engrave pots depicting women in various acts of self pleasure and they even wrote comedies about them! Including one of my favorites: *Aristophane's Lysistrata*, all about a woman who is sexually frustrated and angry about the Peloponnesian War.

I think the Greeks had it right when it came loving is refreshing in comparison to some of the later eras we will talk about.

In the Roman Empire, male genitals were considered extremely lucky. When a general triumphed, he would hang a phallus from his chariot to keep away evil. Elite males had strict rules when it came to sex, one of which was: "One person must dominate while the other must submit." There was never equality in sex. Their caste system was equally strict and affected their sexual unions.

Much like the Greeks, the Roman male thought it commonplace to have multiple partners of both sexes and a wife. Adult citizens were above the riff raff and were the penetrators when it came to same sex relationships; if they were nobles then they would

Saint Augustine's statue—holding a burning heart in hand Charles Bridge in Prague Czech Republic.

be the penetrator to the citizen and so forth. Roman men were free to seek companionship with prostitutes or willing partners. The only trouble they could get into was if it was the respectable wife, son, or daughter of another citizen or noble. Slaves were the lowest of the ranks and bought for their sexual uses as well as their domestic ones.

In the third century, Constantine allied with the Christian Church and they began to place more emphasis on virginity and chastity than ever before. St. Augustine lived the life of a secular Roman male taking in all of the earthly pleasures Rome had to offer. When he took up the Monastic life, he prayed to God. "Give me chastity, but not yet!"

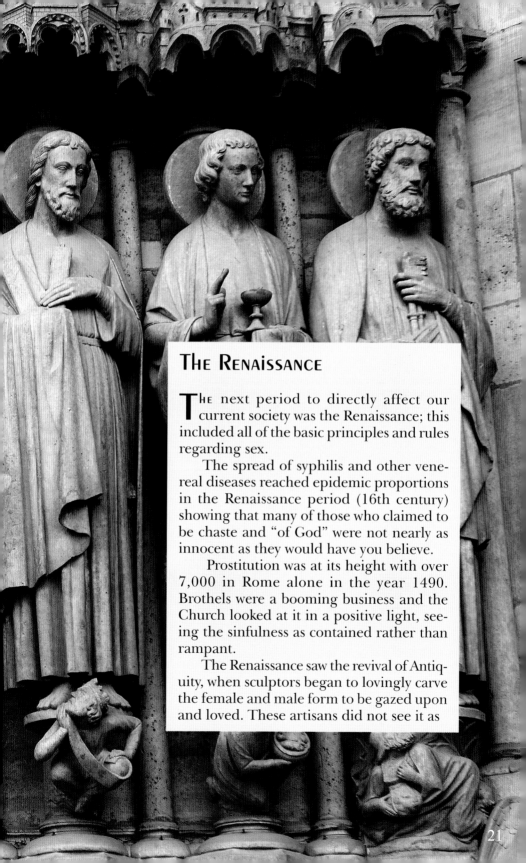

The Renaissance

The next period to directly affect our current society was the Renaissance; this included all of the basic principles and rules regarding sex.

The spread of syphilis and other venereal diseases reached epidemic proportions in the Renaissance period (16th century) showing that many of those who claimed to be chaste and "of God" were not nearly as innocent as they would have you believe.

Prostitution was at its height with over 7,000 in Rome alone in the year 1490. Brothels were a booming business and the Church looked at it in a positive light, seeing the sinfulness as contained rather than rampant.

The Renaissance saw the revival of Antiquity, when sculptors began to lovingly carve the female and male form to be gazed upon and loved. These artisans did not see it as

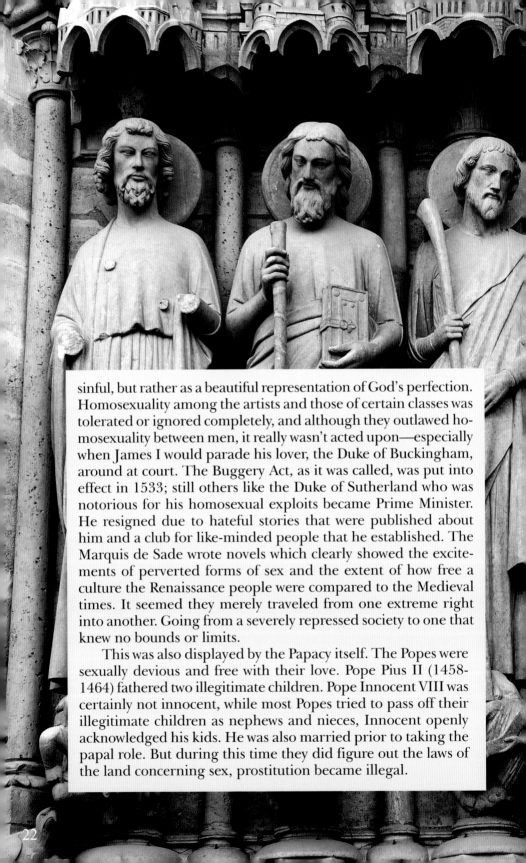

sinful, but rather as a beautiful representation of God's perfection. Homosexuality among the artists and those of certain classes was tolerated or ignored completely, and although they outlawed homosexuality between men, it really wasn't acted upon—especially when James I would parade his lover, the Duke of Buckingham, around at court. The Buggery Act, as it was called, was put into effect in 1533; still others like the Duke of Sutherland who was notorious for his homosexual exploits became Prime Minister. He resigned due to hateful stories that were published about him and a club for like-minded people that he established. The Marquis de Sade wrote novels which clearly showed the excitements of perverted forms of sex and the extent of how free a culture the Renaissance people were compared to the Medieval times. It seemed they merely traveled from one extreme right into another. Going from a severely repressed society to one that knew no bounds or limits.

This was also displayed by the Papacy itself. The Popes were sexually devious and free with their love. Pope Pius II (1458-1464) fathered two illegitimate children. Pope Innocent VIII was certainly not innocent, while most Popes tried to pass off their illegitimate children as nephews and nieces, Innocent openly acknowledged his kids. He was also married prior to taking the papal role. But during this time they did figure out the laws of the land concerning sex, prostitution became illegal.

The Victorian Era

We will move on to the era most closely connected to our own, the Victorians. On the surface, the Victorian Era had to be one of the most prudish societies ever. They were known for their "correct" behavior, Mrs. Mannerly, gaudy Ladies and gallant Lords. Many historical novels romanticize this time period. However, many of the matches made were not for love, but looked at more as a business deal. Sex once a month between husband and wife was the norm. However, for such a sexually repressed society there were undercurrents of sexual perversion and misconduct. In London, a city of almost two million people in 1839, it was found that around 80,000 were prostitutes. It eventually got so bad that the Prime Minister himself would go out to minister and preach to these girls about a different line of work.

The Victorian era was the birthplace of pornography and stroke literature. There were so many rules of etiquette regarding life and interactions with the opposite sex and the act, stroke literature and pornography were only a couple of the many ways they found to rebel.

Homosexuality was looked upon with extreme disgust, and yet Victorian pornography contains various forms of both heterosexual and homosexual love. Shakespeare was not allowed to be read to young girls since they considered him too explicit. However, in 1818 Dr. Bowdler created *The Family Shakespeare,* basically a clean-cut version of the Shakespeare scripts so that "a man could read aloud to his daughters with complete confidence."

This hypocritical view of sex has had long-lasting repercussions on our society. Even to this day we are still very private when it comes to sexual practices. I know when I give readings and begin to talk of the sex act between couples, I still see thirty- and forty-year-old couples who blush. Evidence of the repressive sexual traditions that the Victorian Era has marked us with. I think showing the path of where we came from sexually is important to all of us, that way we can learn real freedom from our inhibitions and recognize sex as a natural and beautiful process meant to be celebrated.

Who Are You in The Bedroom?

We talked in the earlier chapter about the man's role and the woman's role. Well what is *your* role in the bedroom? What about *after* you have sex? Are you someone who likes to snuggle? Are you an adventurous partner?

I believe that every action we take, everything that we do, both in and out of bed, has some form of meaning. So I am going to share with you the knowledge I have gathered over the years. These insights have helped my clients repeatedly realize the disruptions in their lives as a couple and the way they are attempting to let their partner know something is either wrong or right.

First let's talk about your style!

What type of lover personality do you have? I have narrowed it down to four different types, each having their own completely different style. Take this short test to find out what type of lover you truly are.

"The intimacy in sex is never only physical. In a sexual relationship, we may discover who we are in ways otherwise unavailable to us, and at the same time we allow our partner to see and know that individual. As we unveil our bodies, we also disclose our persons."

Dr. Thomas Moore
"Soul Mates," *Psychology Today*

Are you willing to take a chance or try something new? Then you would be the Adventurer.

What's Your Style?

1. You and your partner have had a heated argument in which you were clearly in the wrong and you've left things on a negative note. To make amends you.....

   a. Pretend it never happened and move on.

   b. Let things cool off, and try to look at things from your partner's perspective.

   c. Send flowers and an apology or go back, take your partner to bed in hopes that showing the affection will smooth things over.

   d. You think of something really wacky and out there (such as hiring a belly dancing messenger) to deliver your apology and bring some laughter to your partner.

2. After a bout of passionate sex you...

   a. Take a hot shower alone.

   b. Give yourself five minutes and start again.

   c. Check in on how your partner feels emotionally and physically, maybe even cuddle.

   d. Start coming up with ideas for the next bout of sexual fantasy.

3. Sex to you is....

   a. A way to get out of your own head.

   b. A way to get a feeling of connectedness and understanding of the world on a deeper level.

   c. A blending of energy on a spiritual level.

   d. A way to express and explore the deepest parts of yourself.

4. When it comes to setting the scene for seduction you....

   a. Don't seduce at all.
   b. Openly talk to your partner about their likes and dislikes so that you can set the stage.
   c. Plan everything to make it perfect for your partner.
   d. Pick out your partners favorite fantasy and push it to the limits.

5. You are on a blind date with the perfect partner. If this was the case, their personality would be...

   a. Very open about their life and agrees to things easily.
   b. Confident and very intelligent.
   c. Sexually unintimidating and easy to talk to.
   d. Mysterious and slyly sexual.

Now total the number a, b, c, and ds, then read below to see what who you are in the bedroom!

_____ a

_____ b

_____ c

_____ d

Mostly A's — The Taker

When you are having a sexual relationship with this personality, it may be hard to gain your own pleasure. Unfortunately, with Takers they are the opposite extreme of the Comforter. The name says it all. They often feel that sex is all about the end result. They typically rush things and do not spend as much time enjoying the body and stimulation. Outside of the bedroom, these types have a tendency to be emotionally closed off and a little selfish. Takers are usually very protective of their significant other.

On the upside, they always go after what they want and usually have a determination that can bust through walls and life's obstacles.

Mostly B's — The Seeker

It is not simply about sex; it is more than that for the seeker. Through sex, they often try to find the meaning of life, or to reaffirm the fact that they are living. The Seeker will drown in the pleasure that both partners attain, and constantly look for validation both in and out of the bedroom. They try to be the best at absolutely everything they do, so this personality makes an excellent lover. However, in relationships they may be a little high maintenance.

Mostly C's — The Comforter

This type of lover is all about their partner's pleasure. Sometimes they do not even bother reaching their own climax. Sex is a pacifier. If you are having a time of high emotion, the Comforter will use sex to bring you back to center and avoid having to deal with the issue at hand. Pleasure matters, but not as much as the distraction that it brings. The Comforter is particularly sensitive. Outside of the bedroom, they are the type to have a problem saying no to people and prefer meaningful talk to arguments, Comforter personality types are non-confrontational.

Mostly D's – The Adventurer

Laying in the bed is simply not enough. The Adventurer takes risks in all things that they do, including life. They will try anything once, twice if they are not quite sure. Everything is a game to this personality and they set the rules. One thing is for certain, you will always have fun with an Adventurer. They are spontaneous and go at everything with 110% effort and relish. The Adventurer is more apt to take multiple partners. If you can find a way to tame this personality by keeping up with their needs and curiosities, then you will be in for a wild, fun-filled ride!

Each type has its positive points and its negative ones. The reason this identification of your personality so important is because it is one more piece of a puzzle for both you and your partner. Some clients that come to my table have no clue as to what type of lover they actually live with. They have no idea if the person is a giver or a taker, if they use sex as a tool for avoidance or if they merely love the adventure of it all. Identifying your personality helps both parties to understand what it is you are both looking for out of the sex relationship.

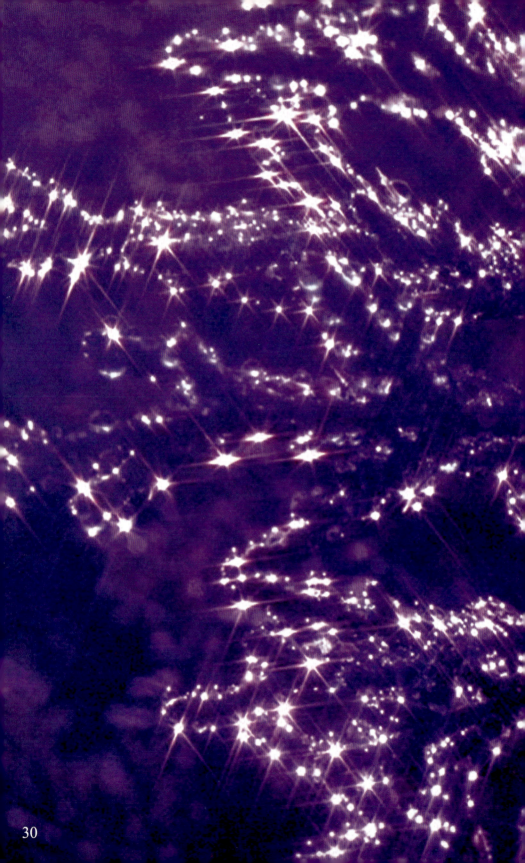

Creating A Complete Psychic Sex Connection

Before we can delve into what a Psychic Sex Connection truly is we must understand how our bodies, mind, and energy work and interplay during the act of sex. Within the body there is one single nerve, but that one nerve branches off like a tree with over a billion offshoots. This is why pressure points are so successful, when you pinch or apply pressure to one of the branch's offshoots—in one part of the body it causes a reaction to the main nerve. Certain kisses and touches can cause the same reaction and oftentimes can trigger both physical and emotional responses. Energy works in much the same way. But first let's focus on the physical reactions.

How Our Bodies Work

So, how exactly does the body work? We are going to need a bit of an anatomy lesson. There are obvious erogenous zones on men and women: genitals, bust/chest, anus. However, the less explored areas such as the neck, knees, and feet can also drive your partner in your mutual pursuit of passion. Please look at the photo of the female. In it, I have shown some of womankind's most sensitive and stimulating erogenous zones! Granted every female is different, and it is definitely worthwhile to explore every area and create your own map to her pleasure.

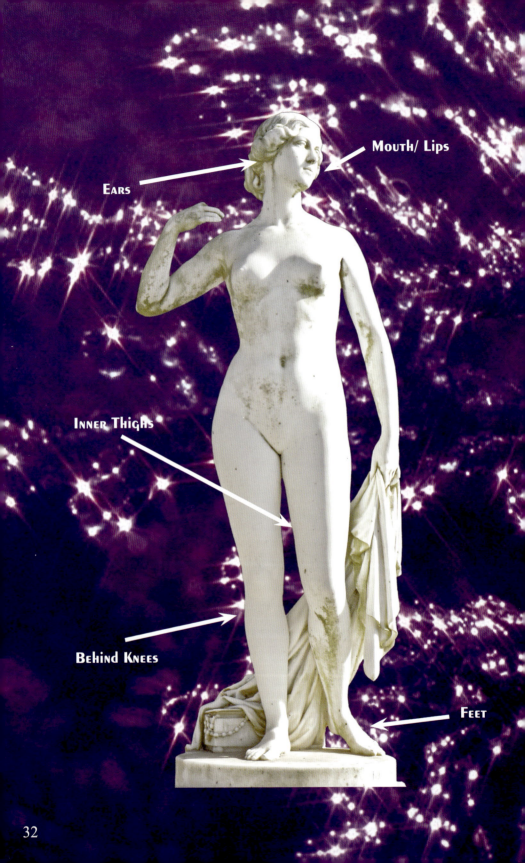

The Woman's Body

REMEMBER, women are much harder to arouse; typically the mind, the body, and heart need to be in complete alignment and agreement prior to lovemaking in order to make it a thoroughly satisfying experience. The body is just one piece of the puzzle.

Ears: Women love it when you just breathe into their ears, licking, and nipping also can create shivers down their spine.

Mouth/Lips: This is the number one erogenous zone for most women. If you can give them, a good kiss, playing with your tongue, nibbling on their top and lower lips, this will rev their engines.

Inner Thighs: Do not bite in this area, it is too sensitive for that, licking, kissing and even a little tickling is just enough.

Behind Knees: It is so overloaded with nerve endings here, but you have to be careful. You don't want the sensation to get annoying or too ticklish (it does not take much to do either), so spend only a couple of minutes. Scraping your teeth lightly over the flesh, licking and nibbling are all acceptable.

Feet: Personally, I think every part of the human body is beautiful in its own sometimes-weird way. Feet to me are the epitome of that thought. They are so filled with vibrant and sensitive nerves. Even feet must be treated like royalty from time to time. Sucking on toes, licking the instep, nipping on the heel, will definitely drive your lover crazy!

The Man's Body

A man's sexuality is as external as a female's in internal (on so many levels). Engaging the body of a man is to engage his mind. Earthy and present, giving a man a rough touch or a passionate kiss in one of his erogenous zones is sure to get him going. The ears, mouth, and inner thighs work on both sexes, as well as lips. However, men have a couple of differences.

Scalp: With all those little nerve endings, the scalp is not to be forgotten! I encourage massaging the scalp on both partners as it opens up the crown and third eye. While it does not cause intense pleasure, it is a wonderful way to relax your partner if they get tense prior to sex and to show them a little extra love. Splaying your hand over the crown of their head and then with medium pressure raking your fingers, back up is very enjoyable for both men and women, using this same motion go all the way around the scalp. Your man will be pleased.

Chest: Every man is different. I remember one client of mine telling me that her husband's nipples were so ticklish that she could not play with them. It would take him right out of the mood. Nevertheless, for those of you who are allowed full access, the chest is a virtual wonderland of assorted delights! Nipping, biting, sucking, and massaging the chest area will bring loads of satisfaction and pleasure to your partner.

Perineum: This is the space between the scrotum and the anus; it will feel soft and sponge like. By massaging this area, you can bring intense pleasure to your man and it helps to open their Root Chakra. Try using a little massage oil or lubricant when you play with this area, as it is extremely sensitive.

How Our Minds Work

I want to talk about the mind for a couple of reasons. Firstly, it is important in any relationship to be stimulated on all fronts, but also I am still seeing that we are inhibited when it comes to voicing our sexual desires aloud. Most of our stresses also come from our mind; we are always waiting for the next shoe to drop. Bills, kids, school, and just life in general can be overwhelming. This can also affect our sex life and connection with our partners. Too many times have I seen a woman sitting at my table questioning her relationship simply because she and her partner are so overwhelmed with life that they don't get enough time together. When they do, it's to talk about their stresses. What about spending some time simply not thinking at all? Is it possible to reach a blank mind state? Yes, it very much is!

Before we get into all of that though, I did want to talk about the true power of the mind just a little bit, have you ever heard of a thinking-off? Dr. Barry Komisaruk, Professor of Psychology at Rutgers University, has been doing quite a bit of research on the matter. He has found that quite a few women (and fewer men) have the ability to actually think themselves into orgasm without ever touching their bodies. "We know that if you think about the clitoris or think about the G-spot or think about the cervix that the corresponding part of the brain map, that those parts of the body become activated."

Using near real time brain imaging he has begun to show these women their scans as they begin to produce their activation of within their genital regions. He equates it to moving your finger, and believes that one day this could help women with spinal injuries that can no longer feel their vagina or enjoy sex.

"We don't really know how far we can go with that. But it's a new approach," says Dr. Komisaruk. I just think it is one more reason why the brain is just so darned cool. Imagine what we will be able to do ten, even twenty, years from now.

Clearing the Mental Clutter

As I was saying, who's mind does not run a million miles a minute? Kids, work, school, bills. It's just bound to keep your mind ranting and raving day and night. To create a true Psychic Sex Connection you cannot have that, so I'm going to give you the tools to help you quiet your mind, so that when it comes time to focus on your partner, you can do that completely, sincerely, without anything getting in the way. If you have bought this book, then on some level you are looking to explore your gifts, your energy, and you are working towards an intimacy you have never before experienced. These following exercises are essential!

The Janitor

Do this meditation whenever you think of it, all throughout the day. It takes time to reach a consistent blank mind state so do not get frustrated; just understand it is part of the process.

Close your eyes see the blackness behind the lids. It is a total darkness, look around you, feel the floor beneath your feet, and you are safe. Listen to the thoughts racing in your mind, see them land on the floor in brilliant white lettering, anything you think, feel, or see ends up on the floor.

As you look to your left a broom sits in the corner; a janitor picks up the broom and begins sweeping up your words like dust. As you continue to think of all of your issues the janitor continues to sweep them up, making them disappear.

You may not reach blank state the first time or even the second but the more you work with the meditation the better off you are. I also suggest doing this before attempting to help your partner with their energy and chakra systems. There are some great breathing techniques you can do with your partner and this next one is simple but effective, really bringing a sense of peace, connection and unification. In order to get the most out of any of these practices, make sure that you do not attempt them when you are tired. This is not something to do late at night right before bed. (The Janitor, you can do at anytime.) Make a point to set aside time daily, or at the very least, three times a week, to reap as much of the benefit from the following exercises as possible.

Deep Breathing (Abdomen)

Sit facing your partner, your back straight and your legs crossed. Alternatively, you can sit in chairs facing each other. Place your left hand on your chest and your right on your abdomen, have your partner do the same. Breathe in through your nose to the count of five, your chest should only move a little and stomach should expand greatly, breathe out through your mouth to the count of five. Do this two more times, once you both get the idea of how the deep breath is supposed to feel join hands with your partner. Look deeply into each other's eyes and begin the deep breathing. Focus on the breath.

Variation: One thing I love to do with couples is what I call *cycled breathing*. You must remember that air is energy; take parts of your partner into yourself by alternating your breathing, you breathe out, and he or she breathes in.

Humor

Laughter is the best medicine for stress. Dr. Lee Burke and Dr. Stanley Tan, from Loma Linda University of Medicine, created carefully controlled studies that showed the effects of laughter on stress chemicals such as cortisol. Dr. Lee summed it up by saying, "If you took what we

Humor really is the best medicine to ease aches, pains, illness, and arguments.

now know about the capability of laughter to manipulate the immune system, and bottled it, it would need FDA approval."

Laughter can do more than just diminish stress; it can also help to boost our immune system. When we stress the cortisol that is released, we can actually cause our immune system's power to decrease. Because of this, when we laugh (thereby diminishing the cortisol), it can help to empower our immune system. I once met a Micmac elder and he said to me, "Before attempting any serious undertaking, we laugh first. It cleanses us of bad energy." I think this is true for anything, whether it be nerves or anger. Laugh for a minute and see what happens. It has also been shown that laughter can change our perspective during stressful situations. It can actually cause us to think that the obstacle we face are challenges instead of burdens.

Hashing Out Issues

It is so important to be sure that you get rid of all of your negative energy before going into the Psychic Sex Connection. If you cannot stop thinking negatively or are having a depressing day, do not have sex in that day. You have to remember that when you orgasm, that is the height of energy release.

There is nothing more powerful on this earth in terms of energy. So if you are thinking negatively, feeling depressed, or doubting the relationship, you immediately throw that energy out there into the Universe. You need to keep communication between you and your partner open at all times. Freedom of expression is so important and if you don't keep the conversation going and check in with each other often, then eventually resentments will build.

Arguments are actually a positive and helpful thing if done correctly. They can allow us to see aspects of our partners we never knew existed. They keep us separate from our partners as well. So many of my clients lose their identities in relationships because they act like a doormat to their mate, doing whatever needs to be done and taking whatever advice, opinion or order that is given. Arguments remind us that even though we love the other person, we are individuals with our own feelings and beliefs. When I'm gearing up for an argument with my hunny, I always point to the ground rules that we have. It is important to respect boundaries on both halves—it's very similar to having a verbal wrestling match. You want the fight to be one hundred percent fair. These are the eight commandments for arguing in my household:

The Eight Commandments For Arguments

1. Thou shall not get physical.

    No slamming doors, no punching walls, kicking animals, or hitting people.

2. Thou shall take responsibility for thy own crap!

    If you are feeling bad about something your spouse says, try to see why it hurt or upset you so much. Yes, sometimes a person's words can be cutting, but how we react to them is our own issue. One thing that I ask my clients to do is takes responsibility for their words by using "I" statements. An example of this would be "I feel like I'm being taken advantage of....." You own that it is how YOU feel, see, or experience something. How you feel and what is fact are two completely different things. Using "I" statements are the easiest way to actually overcome an argument! Oftentimes it bottoms out right there as your partner realizes either that they were in the wrong, or they were in the right and it was merely misinterpreted.

3. Thou shall be completely honest.

    Do not hold back what you feel. Don't try to minimize; be completely gut wrenchingly honest about things. It is important for you to express yourself in order to rid yourself of the negativity.

4. Thou shall not use dirty words against thy partner.

    Don't get nasty and use name calling—that is what happens when someone runs out of steam. If you just need to vent about something else, then go ahead and do that. But don't take out your daily collective stress on your partner and argue for the sake of getting some excess energy out and making yourself feel better by verbally kicking them.

5. **Thou shall get to the point.**

   Too often I see clients beating around the bush when it comes to the problem, drumming up things from years ago! Talk about the now; what is it that really set you off? Also being direct means that you state your case and let the other person talk. Don't ramble just for the sake of wanting to get more speech time. Be slow with this though, especially if it is a deeply traumatic or difficult thing to talk about. Give yourself plenty of time to try to articulate your thoughts.

6. **Thou shall call half-time.**

   Be sure to take a break if the argument gets to be too heated. If you do not, you will not really be hearing each other, you will just be reacting and that solves nothing. It does not mean the argument has stopped, but it does accomplish something positive because with the cool down, you both can digest what you have already seen, heard, and learned.

7. **Thou shall be willing to forgive.**

   You don't always need to forget, but forgiveness isn't just for your partner—it's for yourself as well. Forgiving someone actually allows you to release the emotions and anxieties caught up around the situation.

8. **Thou shall not go to bed angry.**

   No matter what you do, do not bring your problems to bed with you. If you cannot solve them that day, then resolve to put them away that night. That means let go of all of the issues until the next morning.

An Exercise in Communication

There are great ways to communicate, help let go of issues and to hash out negative problems. Here are a couple of exercises to try out.

You and your partner should each sit in a chair facing each other. Take their hands in yours and say to them, "I honor your words as your truth and will respect them as you respect mine." Have them repeat the same phrase. Be sure there is sincerity. Open your heart to hearing what your lover is really trying to tell you, not just the words coming out of their mouth but the feelings behind them. Look them directly in the eye as you let them speak. If there are issues to hash out here is how it should play. Remember to use your "I" statements as in the below role playing example:

LACEY: I feel that you put too much pressure on me when it comes to paying the bills and making the money. I see that you go out all of the time spending the funds that I bring in. Meanwhile, I cannot even buy lipstick for myself because I'm too busy taking care of the kids.

BEN: I hear what you are saying, Lacey, and I respect your outlook. However I must disagree. I see you rarely if ever and I am often at home taking care of the kids. I sympathize that the bills and a job can be overwhelming, but please look at my position. I feel like less of a man because I have to take care of the kids and let you handle everything. I feel that the only time I get away is when I go to do the shopping. I apologize if you feel that you have to shoulder all of the burden. But I would like to see you recognize my contribution to this relationship too.

LACEY: I understand what you mean, and maybe things are harder for you than I thought. I apologize for assuming your job was easy. I know it isn't, I think I just need some time to let off some steam. Is there any way that we can compromise?

BEN: Sure, I think there is, on one of your days off we can maybe hire the girl downstairs to watch the kids and then go and do things together. I think we need to spend more *us* time together....

You can also use this technique much like the Heart Chakra technique to tell each other how much you love each other or things that you do not necessarily like about each other and would like to see changed. We will use the characters Ben and Lacey again.

BEN: I feel horrible when you boss me around.

LACEY: I don't feel I boss you around, however I do see that sometimes you struggle with tasks that need to get done. I just see it as my way of helping you....

One of the things I love most about using "I" statements during arguments is that it tends to quickly diffuse any real anger and brings about a sense of clarity and understanding. Like trying to learn anything new, don't expect it to stick the first time around. I would be surprised if you didn't fall back into old habits. However, with perseverance and repetition comes success. One thing I usually suggest to my clients is the creation of a code word for when one or the other person is slipping back into old habits. Make this a word that you do not often use such as *orange* or *calculator*.

A Cleansing

Letting go of negative feelings can be difficult, especially those deep-rooted ones. I've always loved to write letters, books, poetry and I found for me that continuing to do so was the easiest way to release these tumultuous emotions. Try writing a letter to yourself or to the person you felt you were offended by, pour all of your anger, sadness and hurt into it. Now fold the letter three times however you would like. Hold the letter in your left hand, grab a lighter and head to the bathroom.

As you burn the letter simply state,

> With the energy of fire, I cleanse myself of these burdens. I give myself permission to move on.

Repeat the phrase until you hold nothing but a small corner of the paper then drop it in the toilet. As you flush simply state,

> Water is cleansing and it is rebirth, let the water cleanse me of my burdens so I may be reborn. I give myself permission to move on.

This works on a psychological level giving you physical proof of your release stimulates your belief that you have actually let it go. What you think is reflected in your energy, so now where wounds or holes may be seen in your energy and aura, a light scar may appear or nothing at all. This is a wonderful way to help heal broken relationships if done with your lover or partner in sincerity. It is not important that you read the letter or that you have the other person read their letter to you. It does not matter what it says. All that matters is the emotions poured into it.

Forgive

Another way to help release past negative emotions is to forgive. Like I said in the how to argue properly portion, the only person you hurt when you hold a grudge is you. The person who wronged you does not feel your pain, it does not motivate you in any other way than to continue to let that negative emotion fester until it consumes.

Part of the healing process is understanding situations as they truly are. I have had people wrong me in the past, many times, but still I forgive. Compassion demands that we forgive those who wrong us; it happens for a reason. Some people mistake my compassion for weakness. Compassion is not being weak. Compassion is to understand, to empathize; it is to see the pain the other person must be enduring for them to lash out as they do.

I met a scientist once, and we were talking about karma. I explained to him my idea about how karma works; of course, what you put out there gets returned in a magnified way. We run through the same scenarios with different characters throughout our lives so we can learn our karmic lessons and grow. He did not believe me (surprise). I wasn't looking for his belief, simply to introduce a new idea. Anyway, I asked him if something tragic happened to him recently. He said, "Yes. My mother died." I asked him if he knew that there is a theory or rather a belief in the spiritualist and psychic communities that before the next reincarnation we plan everything out. That what he was going through was a part of his karmic lesson and that this experience would benefit him and someone else later in his life. He of course came back with, "She was almost eighty. Of course she died." Although the pain was still evident, I knew he was not willing to hear what I had to say. I explained to him my ideas, that soon he would meet someone who will also lose a mother or female relative and it would be a "right place, right time" scenario. Darn it, if I did not get a call three months later, his ex-girlfriend had returned home because her mother died and he was there to comfort her and they both found healing because of it.

Therefore, things happen for a reason, understanding that your trauma will help someone else in the future is really an important part of it. It allows you to forgive, and when you see someone else going through a similar thing, it helps you to understand not just that there are others out there. It gives you a way to look at things objectively.

Dirty Words (The Art of Sex Talk)

Ever watch porn? I really do not care for the stuff, but the words, well, those have power. Aside from the look of forced ecstasy on many of the adult entertainers' faces, the words such as "Do me." "Harder, faster." These words, spoken passionately, resonate with us. I've always been a literary fanatic, and I love hearing people's stories. So I guess it would be no surprise that "dirty" words would be a part of this book.

Hypnosis works for one reason and one reason alone, the words—the way they are spoken, the pitch, the formation of each syllable puts us into a deeper place of trance. Certain words hit us. That is why word association games are so much fun! Why don't we try one.

Dirty Word Association

I am going to give you a list of words to get your started. Sit down with your hunny and choose one of you to be the speaker. The speaker will also be the scribe in this game, writing down the word said and what the other partner associated with that word. The other partner will react to the words that are spoken. They say the first thing that pops into their mind when the word is spoken, they are not allowed to think. When you and your partner have gone through this small list (or an expanded one if you want to add more to it), then switch roles.

sex   dildo   masturbate   cum   hard-on

Continue on thinking of any words that might sound "dirty" to you. Word Association has long been used by psychologists to find the link between words and the subconscious. Another variation to this game is to start with one dirty word and play off of each other. This can really be helpful especially if you or your partner are having problems with certain bed room practices or intimacies.

There is another variation of the game where you both build upon the words. For example, Karen and Joe decide to play this variation. Joe is the first speaker:

Joe: Sex

Karen: Love (Karen's affiliation with sex is love)

Joe: Hate (Joe's first affiliation love is its opposite...hate)

You keep going until you run out of steam. One of the great things is you can even make this a real sexy game by setting a prize for the person who uses the last word (say your partner runs out of associations); spice it up and play for "favors." At the same time, it gives you an idea of how you both think, what are the differences and similarities. Oh, and there is only one real rule to this, you cannot repeat a word. Good luck!

Mental Stimulation

WOMEN need time to simmer when it comes to sex; they need to be stimulated in all areas. Guys, on the other hand, while they enjoy being mentally stimulated, it is knowing that the act is going to come to fruition that really gets them going. So this will be torture for both of you in a very pleasurable way. One thing many men don't understand is that you cannot typically just walk up to your girlfriend or wife and whisper raunchy nothings. Although sometimes that will arouse her, setting the mood is incredibly important. If she is feeling particularly unsexy that day, make a point of telling her how much you like the way her hair is or that you think her bum looks awesome in the jeans she is wearing. Be chivalrous! Open doors, move out chairs, yes it's a little bit of work, but believe me it goes a long way.

Most women have become uncomfortable with this kind of behavior. We have become so used to doing things for ourselves that we forget. Remind your woman! Part of the reason I suggest this is because your actions throughout the day will lower her guard for that afternoon or evening. Whisper softly in her ear (see the effects of whispering in a woman's ear under How Our Body Works). Tell her what you plan to do to her, not what you want or what you think you might, but what you plan to do. Saying it as an absolute shows you as the aggressor, and as much as women like to take the lead, when it comes to sex, it is one of the only times they don't have to be in one hundred percent control.

Women, many of us seem to still lack the inhibition necessary to tell our lovers what we like or want! Be vocal about your needs. Most men say they like it when women give them feedback. But more importantly it is a great tool for seduction, picture it, being at a holiday gathering and you're alone in the kitchen getting a couple of drinks. You boldly say to him, "Do you remember last Christmas..." describe for him in detail your best sexual memory, your favorite position or touch. Foreplay like this will get you both hot and quickly, but the point in this is not to go straight to the bedroom but to draw it out, a day, maybe two, of you teasing and flirting and building up that sexual energy. When the moment finally comes, it will be beautiful and well worth the wait!

Remember, when you do communicate to your lover, be good with the detail don't just say, "I like it doggy style." Say, "When you mount me from behind, you hit all of the right spots. It drives

SEX

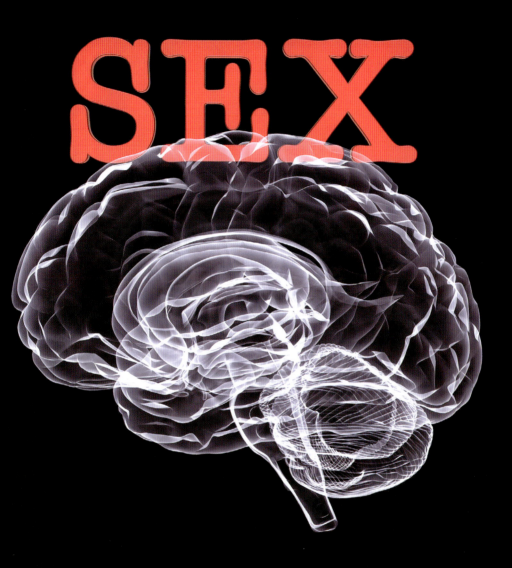

me absolutely insane. I can feel every part of you inside me." This will trigger for both of you the memory of being together and could actually create physical stimuli because of it.

You have to love the mind.

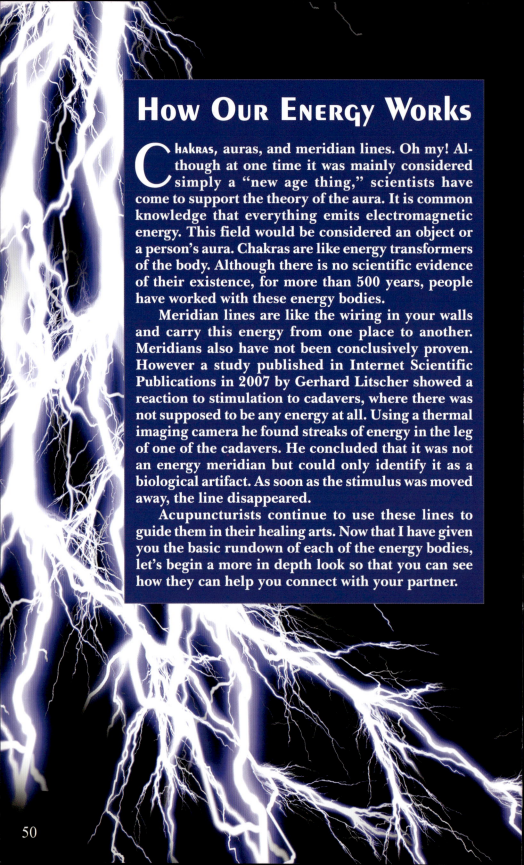

How Our Energy Works

Chakras, auras, and meridian lines. Oh my! Although at one time it was mainly considered simply a "new age thing," scientists have come to support the theory of the aura. It is common knowledge that everything emits electromagnetic energy. This field would be considered an object or a person's aura. Chakras are like energy transformers of the body. Although there is no scientific evidence of their existence, for more than 500 years, people have worked with these energy bodies.

Meridian lines are like the wiring in your walls and carry this energy from one place to another. Meridians also have not been conclusively proven. However a study published in Internet Scientific Publications in 2007 by Gerhard Litscher showed a reaction to stimulation to cadavers, where there was not supposed to be any energy at all. Using a thermal imaging camera he found streaks of energy in the leg of one of the cadavers. He concluded that it was not an energy meridian but could only identify it as a biological artifact. As soon as the stimulus was moved away, the line disappeared.

Acupuncturists continue to use these lines to guide them in their healing arts. Now that I have given you the basic rundown of each of the energy bodies, let's begin a more in depth look so that you can see how they can help you connect with your partner.

Chakras

There are different trains of thought when it comes to chakra systems but I am going to show you the most popular which consists of just seven energetic transformers instead of others which can include up to seventeen if not more. The chakras run parallel to the body and are often seen by alternative healers and Reiki practitioners to be a soft swirling light or wheel. As you can see on the picture there are seven of them each one dictates a different area of the body and has their own function. The chakra system starts at your base or root (genital area). Chakras can move out of balance, get filled with energetic gunk, and begin to spin backwards. This can cause adverse health effects and cause you to feel literally off balance. Most people who work with the chakra systems support them being a little closed, so that you are less sensitive to the things around you, we want you wide open when you are getting ready for a Psychic Sex Connection. It is important to keep your chakras in balance and clear, what better way than sex! As you work with this book you will become more sensitive to the energies and it will be easier for you to tell when you or your partner is out of balance.

Root Chakra

Color: Red

Function: Survival, stability, adds support to the body's system

Aids and Effects: Bones, teeth, nails, colon, prostate gland, rectum, blood and blood cells

Psychic Function: Empowerment, passion, creative energy, courage, strength, motivation

Astrological Correspondence: Aries, Scorpio

Stone: Garnet, Ruby, Onyx, Obsidian

Cleansing the Root Chakra (Couples): Arousing your partner and bringing them to climax is the easiest way to cleanse the root chakra. Although I would not suggest full-blown sex to do this as you must be very conscious of what is happening while you help them. To determine whether or not their chakra is blocked or off center hold your palms over their genital area about 3 or 4 inches above it. Almost like holding a ball keep your hands parallel to each other palms facing. Now see between your palms a bright red ball of energy. This is your partner's chakra. How does it feel to you? Warm and radiant? Light and airy or heavy? If it feels heavy then there is a definite need for work done on this chakra.

Take a deep breath and visualize a red colored ball of light above your head, see it grow from a pinpoint speck into a ball about the size of a balloon. Bring that ball of light down into yourself, see yourself begin to glow a faint red. See the energy work its way down to your hands, then shoot out into the chakra. See the chakra begin to glow brighter and spin clockwise. It may start out slow then it will begin to pick up the pace. Faster and faster, you feel the chakra lighten in weight and move more fluidly. When you have reached this point the chakra is considered clear, open, and ready to work!

The other variation to this is of course pleasure. Instead of holding your hands apart, begin to pleasure your partner, do so slowly letting the energy of the climax build. As you pleasure them envision that red ball. See it coming down to you, as your partner's pleasure continues to increase, see their sexual energy like a while light. It flows into that chakra, mixing with the red energy you have pulled from the Universe. As they reach their climax see the chakra like a bomb release all of the negative or stale energy trapped inside, as it subsides the chakra should be quickly spinning clockwise.

Cleansing the Root Chakra (Individual): As I said in the couple's portion, climax is the easiest way to cleanse your root chakra. This may be a little bit more difficult as you must do both the concentration and releasing. As you pleasure yourself feel your energy build. Go slowly so that it takes at least five minutes for the whole thing. See your sexual energy like a white light building up inside you. As you release send that energy down to your bright red Root Chakra over your genitals. See it like a bomb that explodes free the negative or stale energy. As the impact subsides, you should see this beautiful red hue.

Nurturing the Root Chakra: Try painting, writing, singing (God said to make a joyful noise, not necessarily a beautiful one). Expressing your creativity is essential to keeping your Root Chakra clear. Also focusing on exercise such as strength training, which when done correctly makes you feel more empowered. Facing fears is also a wonderful way to keep your chakra clear whether they be big or small.

Sacral Chakra

Color: Orange

Function: Reproduction, desire, sexuality

Aids and Effects: Pelvis, kidneys, womb, bladder, blood, lymph, gastric juices, sperm, adrenaline

Psychic Function: Uplifting attitude, joy, getting rid of life obstacles and emotional walls, fertility

Astrological Correspondence: Leo, Sagittarius

Stone: Coral, Carnelian

Cleansing the Sacral Chakra (Couples): Have your partner lay on their back, place one hand over the area at the top of the hipbones (feel free to rest your hand on them). Slide your other hand beneath them where their tailbone is. Take a deep breath and close your eyes. You should feel some back and forth motion of energy, almost like a boat in the ocean rocking back and forth. If you feel that then their chakra is just fine. If not it is time to go to work!

Visualize a beautiful orange light in between your hands; sit with that for a moment. How does it look to you? It is spinning counter clockwise? Is it filled with icky black goo? Is it just stopped altogether? Imagine a ball of similarly colored energy emanating above your head, it grows and grows until it is the size of a balloon. Visualize it coming into you, until you glow that same orange color. Now that you are filled with that same energy, see it coming down through your hands and blasting into the Sacral Chakra, ridding it of any gunk or stale energy.

Next see the chakra begin to spin clockwise, the energy still pulsates from your hands giving the chakra a push in the right direction. When you are satisfied, that it is spinning correctly and in the right direction, the cleansing of that chakra is done.

CLEANSING THE SACRAL CHAKRA (INDIVIDUAL): Lie on your back and place both palms side by side over the chakra area. See the beautiful orange light between your hands. How does it look to you? Is it out of alignment away from your hands? Or is it spinning counter clockwise? Imagine a ball of similarly colored energy emanating above your head, it grows and grows until it is the size of a balloon. Visualize it coming into you, until you glow that same orange color. Now that you are filled with that same energy, see it coming down through your hands and blasting into the Sacral Chakra, ridding it of any gunk or stale energy.

    Next see the chakra begin to spin clockwise, the energy still pulsates from your hands giving the chakra a push in the right direction. When you are satisfied, that it is spinning correctly and in the right direction, the cleansing of that chakra is done.

NURTURING THE SACRAL CHAKRA: Is relatively simple, keep happy! Getting into physical exercises such as dance, playing lots of games with friends or family. Having honest deep conversation and putting yourself outside of your comfort zone are all ways to nurture and strengthen the Sacral Chakra.

Solar Chakra

Color: Yellow

Function: Acts of Will

Aids and Effects: Lower back, gall bladder, pancreas, liver, spleen, digestive system

Psychic Function: Removing negative thought and bad habits

Astrological Correspondence: Libra, Taurus

Stone: Amber, Topaz, Citrine

Cleansing the Solar Chakra (Couples): We are looking for that same feeling and visual around each of the chakras, grasp this on in the same way that you did the Root Chakra. The Solar Chakra is located at the end of the rib cage (right above the belly button) hold your palms facing each other three or four inches above your partner's body. How does that area feel to you? By now you should get a feeling for chakras and a way to judge. Remember if it feels heavy, or looks like it has stopped spinning then work needs happen.

    Have your partner lay on their back. Take a deep breath and visualize a yellow colored ball of light above your head, see it grow from a pinpoint speck into a ball about the size of a balloon. Bring that ball of light down into yourself, see yourself begin to glow a faint yellow. See the energy work its way down to your hands, then shoot out into the chakra. See the chakra begin to glow brighter and spin clockwise. It may start out slow then it will begin to pick up the pace. Faster and faster, you feel the chakra lighten in weight and move more fluidly. When you have reached this point, the chakra is clear, open and ready to work!

Cleansing the Solar Chakra (Individual): Lie on your back and place both palms side by side over the chakra area. See the beautiful orange light between your hands. How does it look to you?

Is it out of alignment away from your hands? Or is it spinning counter clockwise? Imagine a ball of similarly colored energy emanating above your head, it grows and grows until it is the size of a balloon. Visualize it coming into you, until you glow that same yellow color. Now that you are filled with that same energy, see it coming down through your hands and blasting into the Sacral Chakra, ridding it of any gunk or stale energy.

Next see the chakra begin to spin clockwise, the energy still pulsates from your hands giving the chakra a push in the right direction. When you are satisfied, that it is spinning correctly and in the right direction, the cleansing of that chakra is done.

Nurturing the Solar Chakra: Meditation is an excellent way to work towards reprogramming your brain to positive thinking. I am multi-denominational in my spiritual beliefs, and have a passion for mythological deities. There is one meditation I came up with when I was thirteen or fourteen. It features Anubis, God of Judgment; this helped me a lot when I was being self-critical. In it Anubis plays the role of judge and jury. It is a very cleansing experience.

Self Judgement Meditation

You walk into a tomb, it's tan-colored block walls are cold to the touch but torches warm the room; you follow a passageway deeper into the earth. The steep decline seems to go on forever, the light from the torches cast eerie shadows and you feel as though you are not alone. You come upon a door, its iron handle is cold to the touch. Hesitantly you open it; you enter into a room filled with light. A giant scale lies in the center, and a black dog-headed figure stands to the left of it.

"Why are you here?" he asks in a deep gravelly voice.

"To have my self-judgments weighed," you reply.

"As you will." He approaches you standing to your left. You notice on one side of the scale is a feather on the other is nothing. This is where you judgment will go.

Anubis continues on," If your judgment is true then you will rise higher than the feather, if it proves false you will sink lower. Because truth unburdens us and makes us lighter, lies weigh us down and keep us from growing. Sit upon the scale."

You follow his direction and sit on the right side of the scale, the brass is cold on your buttocks, you tremble a little bit out of nervousness. Then the scale begins to move. You hold on to two of the three chains connected to the plate as the scale balances itself.

After a couple of minutes, you are equal to the feather.

"What is your first judgment?" Anubis asks, his black eyes seem to see through you, into your very being.

"My name is *(insert your name here)*." Slowly the scale moves, you begin to descend, and then ascend.

"Truth, your name is *(insert your name here)*."

"I am not perfect, even though I should be." Your side of the scale moves downward, then up, then down again.

"False, you are perfect. Just as you were meant to be."

"I am to skinny/fat." Your side of the scale stays just as it is.

"False. You are not too skinny/fat."

Continue through your own self-judgments. Let Anubis help you, but please be honest with yourself. You will get nowhere if you do not.

You leave the room closing the heavy door behind you. You walk up the tunnel back towards the main entrance. There is no fear in the tunnel now, only a bright light as if it were day; no shadows leap upon the walls. You enter the main room of the tomb and walk out the entrance and into the light of the day. You will wake feeling refreshed, renewed, rejuvenated and loved.

This is something you are going to want to read over once or twice to get the gist of. Or you can have your partner read it to you. Be sure that their voice remains calm, they do not need to have a "hypnotic voice," simply keeping their voice even will suffice.

The other thing you can do is, when you have a negative thought, back it up consciously with five positive ones.

Heart Chakra

Color: Green

Function: Spiritual Love, Compassion

Aids and Effects: Upper back, breasts, heart, lungs, air circulation

Psychic Function: Self-love and esteem, healing emotional traumas, connecting with inner child

Astrological Correspondence: Aquarius, Cancer

Stone: Peridot, Rose Quartz, Malachite

Cleansing the Heart Chakra (Couples): This chakra is so important, it can help us release our past traumas; bring about a feeling of Universal Connection and more. It is imperative that we keep it healthy and moving. Have your partner lie on their back. Look into their eyes, and let your positive energy shine. Honestly and sincerely tell them how much you appreciate them. Do not break eye contact. Tell him or her all of the positive things you can think of—about their body, nature, mind and soul, any that you can think of. Place your left hand over their heart. Let those positive feelings overwhelm you. As you do, summon that beautiful green energy and see it manifesting inside your own heart. It travels the path to your left hand where it settles beneath your palm into their Heart Chakra. See their Heart Chakra reacting your energy; see it begin to spin and brighten as it absorbs your love.

Cleansing the Heart Chakra (Individual): Look for those positive things within yourself; think of all the wonderful things people have complimented you on. Your favorite features, the best parts of your personality. List all of these things in your mind. Put yourself back to your favorite childhood memory. The point is to focus on something positive concerning yourself. As you bring these feelings to the forefront, place your hand over your heart, visualize a brilliant green energy starting behind your eyes. It's so powerful that everything you look at has a green tint to it. Next see that green glow travelling down, through your throat and down your left arm, finally it lands beneath your palm directly into your Heart Chakra. See it settle there, your chakra absorbs this beautiful green healing energy as it does the chakra begins to spin clockwise, faster and faster. When you feel the chakra has become light, airy and is moving fast enough then stop sending the energy to it.

NURTURING THE HEART CHAKRA: Each chakra is important in its own right, but when it comes to connecting during sex and relationships the Heart Chakra rules over it all. Many of us have emotional triggers that cause us to lash out at those closest to us. It could be a look on your spouse's face that reminds you of the one your mom used to give you when she would deny you something, or your best friend's tone of voice could remind you of kids at school or some other negative event. Those are the times when we react strongly to something that may not necessarily warrant the emotional energy we give it. Being true to your Heart Chakra is to understand these triggers and speaking openly about them. If you get into an argument or have a bad reaction, before you begin attacking, really think about the moment objectively. What is it that this scenario reminds you of? Let your partner or friend know. I did this with one client I had. She and her husband were arguing all the time over the littlest of things, their reactions were always loud and they would get into shouting matches that even the neighbors could hear.

Coming From the Heart

Melissa G. and Larry, were horribly unhappy in their marriage and were considering divorce when Melissa finally decided to come see me. Her husband was of course skeptical. Immediately upon looking at the energy they shared which was like a thick and twisted vine and both of their Heart Chakras were blocked to each other and scarred beyond anything I had seen before. I began getting impressions from both sides. Growing up Melissa dealt with a verbally and sometimes physically abusive brother (who she later ended up taking care of due to alcoholism) and Larry had been through quite a few different relationships but at one point had a severe dressing down by one of his first loves.

I looked pointedly at Melissa, "When he gets mad who does he remind you of?"

"I don't think he reminds me of anyone, it just gets me more riled. Some of the things he yells at me for are nothing. Like doing the dishes or not putting enough gas in the car."

"And who does that remind you of? Think hard." I asked again.

"I don't know." she replied. I cannot say I was really that surprised that she would not bring up her brother, there was such an emotional wall around her. It was like she was waiting for me to side with her against her husband.

"What about the abusive male that was around you? I get a brother figure with it, does that make sense to you?"

"Well, yeah he used to be mean when I was a kid, but he isn't anymore."

"So would it be plausible to say that Larry reminds you of your brother?" Melissa thought about it for a second and then nodded looking away and picking at a few loose strings on her pocketbook. "You know a lot of times, when things trigger us and we take our anger out on the people we feel safe with. Do you feel safe with Larry?"

"Yes. I guess I do," she replied.

"Larry, who does Melissa remind you of when she gets angry or does not do things right?" I asked.

"That's easy, my ex-girlfriend Linda. She used to get on me about doing things the right way. But she would never do them herself, then she would berate me in front of everyone and anyone. It was really upsetting. Sometimes, I just think that I did it again. I got with another Linda, so I lash out," he said casually. A little too easily if you asked me, again there was the emotional wall, hardened heart I guess you would call it. Nevertheless, I saw these two were at the same growth point; their energy even though each had their issues, they had the potential for an awesome open connection.

"Melissa do you recognize the person he is talking about?" I asked.

"Yes, he has mentioned her once or twice, but we never really talked about it. So we figured out who we remind each other of; now what do we do. That hasn't helped anything. I don't feel instantly better."

"No, you don't and you will not. I'm not going to lie to you. There is a lot going on here, but we have a place to start." I said sometimes it is difficult being a psychic and working with couples. It is like they expect a quick fix. Unfortunately, there are so many complexities in the human mind and in the energy therein that it is not a one session deal.

"Try this exercise for me. Remember when you first got together, the wonderful things you first noticed about each other. Now turn your chairs to face each other, Melissa put your left hand over his heart. Larry put your left hand over her heart. Alright, recognize now that you are both intimately connected, the left hand is the one closest to the heart that is why we are using that one. Also recognize that each of you can wound each other easily this way, because whatever you say next will be absorbed by the Heart Chakra."

They both looked at me as if I had nine heads, so I went on to explain the chakras. Even though skeptical at this point, they were ready to try anything, and I knew that alone was what would make this session successful. Remember, if there is still any type of passion on both sides in a relationship, it isn't over. If you feel indifferent, then consider it done.

"Alright, so Melissa, tell Larry some of the first things you noticed about him. Make sure to keep eye contact with him."

"Your eyes, they are a bright green. You tried to be the toughest guy in the room and then when we were alone you would be so romantic. I loved how you stuck up for me and your friends whenever someone tried to bully us. Your loyalty was the first thing that made me love you. I hadn't had that before." Melissa smiled at him

"Now it's your turn Larry." I urged him to be completely open with her.

"Well, first thing I noticed was that you always tried to fade into the background, but it never worked. You have a magnetic personality. When you were happy, it filled you up, your eyes, smile everything. I liked your cool head, and the fact that you didn't want to sit around all day, that you were athletic. I fell in love with you on the camping trip, you, me, Glen and Carly; I was getting off work late and you didn't care. It was one in the morning and you came and got me anyway. You were carefree and such a flirt. I swear sometimes you tried to make me jealous, but it just filled me with pride. I really do love you, ya know." Larry said somewhat sheepishly at the end.

"I know you do. I really want to make it work. I can feel what you're saying, it speaks to my heart." Melissa's eyes softened toward him. Immediately you could start to see the energy change and the walls beginning to come down. Melissa's guard dropped and now was the time to push forward.

"Melissa now is the time to confront the brother that you see in your husband. It is important for you to gain healing in this way so that you do not make your husband pay for the sins of your brother." I looked pointedly at Larry. "And vice versa with your girlfriend."

Next we went through some exercises to help them release the negative energy they had pent up for so long. Part of it was to write a letter to their past abusers, putting in all of their pain, all of their anger, and then burning it and flushing it down the toilet. I find that physical representations are often the best way to get through to the psyche when it comes to releasing negative energy. It affirms in the mind that the subject is truly done and over with, that you have been purged.

They left my office, ready to go out to dinner. I checked in with them a couple of weeks later. I'd sent them home with homework. They were to continue to purge by getting rid of artifacts that may have held a negative representation to them when it came to their abusive pasts. Whether it be something Larry threw in anger or the "comfy shirt" she seemed to always wear when they got into their arguments. My reason behind this was based purely on energy. It is called residual energy and when there are extreme emotions or violent actions, whatever is around at that time will pick up on that energy and act almost like a sponge.

When I checked in with them, they both sounded happy although they admitted to a short relapse. But they said they had conducted the heart to heart exercise, taken five minutes to think and reassess and then realized that they were actually taking a lot of their daily stresses out on each other because they felt safe. As I'm writing this, it has been over a year now since I last had them in my office and I checked in with them just last month.

Melissa and Larry, after years of trying, finally conceived, and they have not had a real argument in almost six months. Universe knows when the energy is right and I guess it was for them. I am always thankful they did not give up.

Daily acts of kindness reinvigorate our Heart Chakras; it can be anything from holding a door to giving a poor man a couple of dollars, as long as you do it with no expectations for a return. True kindness comes from a selfless place. This is what the heart wants, its energy is boundless and needs to be shared, and there is plenty so do not worry about running out.

Throat Chakra

Color: Blue

Function: Communication, creative speech

Aids and Effects: Neck, throat, thyroid, lungs, windpipe, ears.

Psychic Function: Helps in making decisions and dispelling confusion, patience, wisdom, fidelity

Astrological Correspondence: Virgo, Capricorn

Stone: Sodalite, Blue Lace Agate, Lapis, Lazuli

Cleansing the Throat Chakra (Couples): When it comes to the Throat Chakra you need to be very careful. This is your voice we are talking about. Sit on the floor with your legs crossed facing each other. The key of G major is an integral part of the Throat Chakra chant HAM OM HAM. The first note of the G major scale is, of course, G. To find this key go to a piano or even online. It is well known that even those who lack musical ability can tell the difference between major and minor scales, as the major scales are often bright and full sounding, where as the minor scales have a tendency to be sad and haunting. So go find you G major. When you do, play it a couple of times. As you listen, hum the note and feel it vibrate in your throat.

When you feel confident that you have the note, begin chanting HAM OM HAM; feel the throat vibrate as you form the words and the Throat Chakra releasing the negativity and toxins trapped inside. Stare deeply into each other's eyes as you do this. It is both a cleansing and a bonding experience.

Continue this chant for as long as you are comfortable, between ten to fifteen minutes should suffice. I use this mantra all of the time; it brings a sense of peace and helps when you have a habit of stumbling on words. It is also great if you need to confront someone and are looking for a little guidance on how to go about it.

CLEANSING THE THROAT CHAKRA (INDIVIDUAL): Unfortunately, when working on yourself as an individual it is easy to fall back into old routines, so it is important that you have a great support system around you of friend or family. It is ultimately important that you have clear communication with those people, otherwise your Throat Chakra will become blocked. As I said in the couple's section, there is a great mantra for cleansing the Throat Chakra. You may want to burn some lavender and sage to set the mood, light a couple of light blue candles and sit cross legged on the floor or on a pillow. Take three deep breaths in through the nose out through the mouth, bring that breath down to the stomach and then out. Close your eyes and clear your mind. In the key of G Major begin the Throat Chakra chant of HAM, OM, HAM. Feel it vibrate in your throats as it helps the chakra release the toxins and negativity trapped inside. Go for as long as you please, typically ten to fifteen minutes does the trick.

NURTURING THE THROAT CHAKRA: Since we are already getting you into a meditative state I think it is time for another meditation! This one features Hecate Goddess of the Crossroads, she is ever decisive and helps when you are in a bind concerning choices. Sometimes it is hard for us to look at things objective and having your Throat Chakra blocked does not aid; in fact, it may harm your decision-making process. But even with the block removed, that does not mean all of your options will suddenly become clear. That is why I created this exercise:

A Goddess Helps

On the night of the full moon, you leave your home and head for the street corner, two streets intersect with four stop signs. Suddenly a mist descends in the middle of the road. From it comes a beautiful woman, her long red hair has gray streaks at the temples. In her left hand she carries a staff, her dark green cape swirls around her of its own accord. There is no breeze.

A soft smile makes her look younger than her years, "You are one of my favorite creations," she says to you, her voice a lilting symphony of vocal chords. "What can I do for you, my child?"

"I am a stuck Hecate _____, I
   (tell the problem you are facing)
don't know what to do! Can you please show me my options? Aid me in making this decision," you ask, looking to the kindly woman for help.

"I am the Goddess of the Crossroads; I help those who need to choose a path. I am a part of you; you need not fear the choices you make for I lead you to them. Each choice is a lesson, and each lesson is a blessing. Do not fear seeking counsel from me for I am always here." She touches your mind. "Do not hesitate upon making a choice, for that makes the choosing harder, always rely on my voice inside you. I will always point you in the right direction. If it does not turn out the way you planned, it is simply another adventure, another experience, from which to learn, but you are always protected—worry not. These are your choices."

Suddenly the road signs melt away, the red paint dripping off the sign beneath it. On each sign is an option. The street lights flicker and change to different colors. Each street has its own hue: red, green, blue and yellow.

"Each color represents a different path," Hecate tells you. "Which color are you drawn to?"

"_____." Say this color aloud.
  (Name the color)

"Each color has its own representation, my child. You have chosen..." (Skip to the appropriate color.)

Green: Brings healing, but obstacles will be placed in your path to cause that healing to occur.

Blue: Will bring you financial and spiritual security. But you must work twice as hard to keep it.

Yellow: Will bring you the recognition you desire, but you must be open to the opportunity and the sacrifice that may be needed to attain it.

Red: Gives you passion and creativity, but you must learn to harness it and use it wisely, else that passion will be like a fire and consume you.

"I am with you always my child, to guide you through the uncertain threads that Fate weaves. You must realize that the web is merely a guide not a certainty. We make our own way."

The old woman opens her arms to you and you embrace her. It feels as though you are hugging your mother or grandmother, such love and affection, tenderness and acceptance of everything you are. A surety and confidence flows over you.

Suddenly she is gone, but she is not gone; she is a part of you always. You are alone, but not alone. You are your Mother's child and She is always with you.

You begin to walk down the street you have chosen; suddenly it seems as if the Sun has risen it is so bright out and your path becomes clear.

You awake feeling refreshed, rejuvenated, and confident in your choices and decisions.

Clear communication is imperative when it comes to nurturing the Throat Chakra. Remember in your communications to always use the I words. "I think, I feel, I hear, I see." The reason for this is double fold, when it comes to arguments, starting with "I" statements show that you are taking responsibility and less accusative to the person you are talking to. In addition, it helps to honor yourself and feels as though you are truly being heard. This strengthens your Throat Chakra with every word you utter.

"Sex is more than an act of pleasure, its' the ability to be able to feel so close to a person, so connected, so comfortable that it's almost breathtaking to the point you feel you can't take it. And at this moment you're a part of them."

~ Anonymous

Third Eye Chakra

Color: Indigo

Function: Sight, Intuition

Aids and Effects: Face, central nervous system, nose, sinuses, eyes, ears, pituitary gland

Psychic Function: Helps to slow a busy mind, psychic growth, karma, meditation

Astrological Correspondence: Gemini, Sagittarius

Stone: Iolite

Cleansing the Third Eye Chakra (Couples): You will need this exercise if you have fear of your own intuition, do not listen to your gut instincts and deny that part of yourself. The exercise you are about to embark on will help you with the opening and closing of your Third Eye Chakra. The reason I love this exercise so much is that it was one taught to me by my mother, but it also works really well! Instead of seeing it as the indigo energy, we are going to see it like an indigo eye.

Have your partner visualize a third eye in between their eyebrows. Have them visualize it closed, you can hold their hand and lend your own energy to their exercise. First establish a signal between the two of you so that you will be able to let each other know when you have visualized the eye. This could be as simple as saying, "Ready" or "Got it." Then begin working on getting that beautiful chakra eye opened. Slowly see the eye open as you begin to get glimpses of the indigo iris—it glows, gaining power. When it is fully open, a beautiful indigo light blasts from it. Your partner's Third Eye Chakra is now open!

Cleansing the Third Eye Chakra (Individual): The Third Eye Chakra originates from the Hindu, if you look at their god Shiva, you will see he also has a Third Eye. He was well known for his wisdom and foresight. Get ready for some relaxation! Get into the bath or the shower; every time you release a chakra, it is important to cleanse, that is why when I do energy cleansings and chakra realignments I usually do it all at once. Then we do a full cleanse to help rid the last of the negative energy. Think of it like black ooze that your chakras spit out, almost like a pimple. Some people do not realize that even though you cleanse the chakra itself that the actual energy can still be there.

As you soak or shower, visualize a closed Third Eye. It sits vertical in between your two eyebrows just like Shiva's. As you begin to slowly open it, you see the eye has a dull indigo color; the white parts are almost black. It is a little difficult to open the eye, but you continue anyway. As you force it open, the black liquid begins to drain, revealing a beautiful indigo gemstone eye. When you get it fully opened, the light from this eye shines so brightly you see things in shades of indigo. It shoots like a continuous beam of light from your Third Eye. Just sit and let the eye get its bearings; relax and wash away the energetic grime.

NURTURING THE THIRD EYE CHAKRA: To nurture the Third Eye is to accept your psychic self. Meditation is the best way to do this. Psychic development books are great, but I always say go with your own intuition. That is the key to keeping your Third Eye in good repair. Challenge yourself consistently; you can even do it with little things like what color car will drive around the block next. There are many games in my prior book, *Raising Indigo, Crystal and Psychic Kids*, but you can scour the web and find plenty as well. I know one that is a favorite at my house: Guess The Shape. One of us will think of a shape and focus on it. Everyone writes down their answers while the "thinker" writes down and concentrates on the chosen shape. This is called a "sending and receiving" game.

Crown Chakra

Color: Violet

Function: Understanding

Aids and Effects: Brain and pineal gland

Psychic Function: Connection of body and soul, past lives, connection to divinity, justice, forgiveness

Astrological Correspondence: Pisces

Stone: Amethyst

Cleansing the Crown Chakra (Couples): When you work in any kind of psychic field, it is always important to keep your Crown Chakra open. It is the entryway to the Universal energy. When working with sex energy, reaching orgasm is the epitome of manifestation energy that you can summon. So we need to be sure that your Crown Chakra is wide open so that you can send that energy out to be received by Universe and put into action. Buy a piece of amethyst and clear quartz. These are relatively cheap and found at any stone or metaphysical store. Have your partner lie down and place the stone at the top of their head about two or three inches above it. Therefore, the crystals should lie on the ground. The amethyst will help to cleanse the chakra, and the quartz will work as an energy magnifier. Just put them side by side there is no special formation. Have your partner lay there for around twenty minutes or so, burn some beautiful smelling white sage, which is also a cleansing herb. Waft it around them using your hand like a fan; this will help the energy body to expel any negativity or toxins.

Cleansing the Crown Chakra (Individual): Lay down on the floor, or bed and place an amethyst stone above your head, it needn't be large—just a small one is fine—next to that, place a piece of clear quartz. The vibrations of the Amethyst match the Crown Chakra perfectly and will cause it to begin spinning correctly again, lay there for about twenty minutes. This allows the amethyst time to interact with the Crown Chakra, you can also chant the mantra for the Crown Chakra: HUM OM HUM, in the Universal Key of OM. As you do, close your eyes and see the interaction between your beautiful Crown Chakra and the amethyst stone, the quartz merely magnifies the energy of the amethyst causing and interaction of dazzling purplish lights.

I know for me, when I do this exercise, sometimes I get lost in it and what was meant to take twenty minutes can turn into an hour or more. So if you are on a time restriction, I suggest using a timer.

Nurturing the Crown Chakra: Going out to meet new people, celebrating the friends you have, the Crown Chakra is about acceptance, as much as it is about manifestation. It gives us the gift of Understanding, something in our modern day and age that few of us still possess. Understanding goes beyond getting the gist of something or "hearing" someone speak. Understanding is about truly listening to what the person is saying, not just in the words, but beneath them as well. Many who have blocks in their Crown Chakras have a tendency to push people out of their lives instead of inviting more in, so I say invite new people into your home, into your life. Celebrate the friends you have and appreciate them for their perfections and their flaws!

Another way to continue keeping your Crown open is to work continuously at manifestation. My mother used to call it "Wish Magick." Simply think of something you want; feel it in your mind. Say you want a new car because yours is almost dead, see the car you want, envision yourself driving it, feel the interior, hear the stereo, smell that new car scent, manifest it so much in your mind that you would swear it was real. See that manifestation like a ball of purple energy gathering in your mind. Keep holding it until you feel like your head is going to explode. When it gets to that point, shoot it out of your Crown Chakra like a cannon. Then forget about it. That is "Wish Magick." Things may come to you in mundane ways; don't expect to go outside and find your car. there. But something else may happen. For instance, you may end up having a friend who needs to get rid of their car because they are getting a new one and they may want to give it to you for just the right price, or you see an ad in the newspaper that just happens to catch your eye. Either way, appreciate it as more than just coincidence; see it as the gift that it is and move on. Oh, yes, one more thing, DO NOT DOUBT! Negative emotions travel faster than positive ones, so if you doubt, it will not come to fruition. It is better to forget that you ever put a wish out there in the first place.

Using the Chakra Stones

In your daily life, and in psychic sex, you can use the stones to your advantage, increasing the effect of the chakra by wearing the stone it correlates to. For instance, if you are having a hard time concentrating or you are feeling more flighty than usual, you may want to tap into your Root Chakra and strengthen it some by wearing onyx or hematite. If you are feeling less empowered, then again you can strengthen the Root Chakra and gain the extra attributes by wearing garnets or rubies.

If you are feeling down and depressed, wearing carnelian will strengthen your Sacral Chakra giving you a quick pick me up. When you notice that your goals are not being reached, you may want to tap into the power of your Solar Plexus Chakra by wearing citrine a stone of personal power, ambition, and success. Carrying Peridot in the form of jewelry will help to boost the power of your Heart Chakra, opening you up for love; it will also bring you emotional balance and universal consciousness.

Turquoise is a very strong stone heavily connected to the Throat Chakra; it will increase the amount of deep communication helping you to get to the heart of issues with other people! This is a great stone to use when wanting to discuss major issues with your partner. Azurite is a gorgeous stone with great capabilities in the forms of spiritual awareness and psychic development. When you need to get a read on a room full of people or want to know if someone means you harm or help, this is a great one to get as it really does aid in the receiving of vibes from others. Finally, the amethyst, connected directly to the Crown Chakra: Wearing amethyst will not only help to increase your psychic abilities, but it will also help to bring you closer to cosmic consciousness and give you a great energy boost.

Now if you decide to wear these things in the setting of jewelry, you should be aware of the metal that you choose. Let's start with the granddaddy of metals. If you choose to go with gold, aside from being one of the most valued of metals in terms of cost per gram, it also works in tune with the Third Eye and Crown Chakras helping to open you up! Gold also helps with attracting money, healing, and success. I've always viewed gold as an aggressive metal – if you are looking for things to motivate quickly, this is the metal to choose. It's also a great one for protection. Silver is a little bit more subtle; it combines the feminine aspects of the moon in its reflective brilliance. It is a great conductor carrying the energy of the stones directly to the energy of the body, a perfect metal to help you get as much juice from the stones as possible. Lastly, we will talk about copper, which is believed to help protect the body from disease; aside from that, it will also bring love, money, and healing.

Oftentimes, I tell my clients to look for the meaning behind everything and be aware of what they choose. An example of this would be to choose to get an amethyst set in gold. What a combination! Gold, which as we know stimulates and opens the third eye along with amethyst, is renowned for it's ability to psychically open someone making this a one-two punch! However, if we set that same stone into copper, the wearer may get vibes here and there, but then again, it could just fall flat, as the metal does not have that same vibration as gold. So be aware and pay attention!

Chakra Stones.

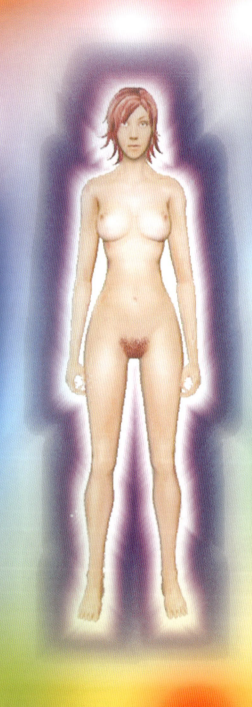

Auras

Have you ever been in a room when someone walks in and it's like everyone notices them? Many people would describe this as an "aura of power." But what is an aura? As I said at the beginning of the section, everything gives off electrical energy and humans are no different. An aura is merely the field given off by our own electrical currents. It changes from minute to minute depending on what or who we are interacting with, our moods, illnesses, etc. Much like chakras, it is important to keep your aura "clean." Many of us can actually end up with holes in our aura, which tells of past trauma. There are ways to fill this in though. The other thing we need to be aware of is, when we become defensive, our aura gets really thin and creates something like a shell. I remember one client's reaction when I got close to a truth he didn't want to hear – his aura got so hard and really dark red. A hard red shell encased him.

Seeing Auras

Every time I have someone sit at my table after the reading is done they always ask, "How do you do that?" Here is the deal: The human mind ... well, we like to overcomplicate things. The psychic world is actually very simple. It is nothing short of minimal as far as actual work is concerned. We each have abilities inside of us; we are each intrinsically connected through our energy to each other, objects, and the energies that create matter. To see these energies is not difficult at all; it is a matter of putting yourself in the ideal situation. At first, and then when you work with it more, much like a muscle it gets stronger, soon enough, you will be able to see auras all of the time!

So what is the ideal situation? What you will need is for your partner to stand against a white wall. White is created from all colors, whereas black absorbs them. This is best done during the day when you can get as much light as possible. Now stand about ten to fifteen steps away from your partner facing them directly. Look just to the left of them, take a deep breath, relax your shoulders and let your eyes soften. You may not see color the first time or the second, but you should see a small outline at first, then almost like heat waves. This is the electrical energy. I suggest trying it not just with people, but plants, animals and objects as well. Everything has energy, so there are no real limits. Keep working it and you will be an aura connoisseur in no time.

Aura Colors

As I said, it may take you a while to see the actual colors, but when you do, I promise it will blow your mind. They are not like natural colors; they are so vibrant, as to be almost alive. Here is a list of the aura colors and what they mean:

White

Many people who see auras actually see the white at the first layer but you can find white in the main aura body as well. Here are some of the colors:

Pure White Light

> High psychic abilities, even though you may have them you may not have tapped into them yet.

Smoky White

> It appears like a thin white smoke within the aura; it signifies a transformation that may seem hard to go through, but it has a positive end result.

Starlight

> This is a wonderful, almost starlit quality to the aura; you see it more around people who are spiritually aware rather than physically aware. In addition, you may see it around those who are about to pass on to the Otherside.

French Vanilla

> Much like the ice cream with its smooth but bold flavors, a French vanilla tone indicates that you are someone who has found their path. You are on the right road and you should stick with it.

Purple

Vibrant Purple

> This color is almost electric in its vivid color. If you see it in the aura, it means this person is exactly where they are

supposed to be at that moment. They are open and attuned to the Universe in all ways.

Plum

The plum is a beautiful and majestic shade and means exactly that. A person with plum in their aura shows new spiritual beginnings. Oftentimes I see the plum shade in relation to creativity and divine inspiration in the arts.

Violet

This is a blue-purple color; it shows a perfect balance between the mind, heart, and body.

Lilac

This softer purple presents in the auras of those who have denied their abilities for an extended period of time; the ability is there, but it has never been nurtured and therefore cannot reach the Violet that many attain to. It also indicates a person who has endless compassion towards all things.

Blue

Indigo

If Indigo is what mainly makes up a person's aura, than this person is an Indigo Child. In my book, Raising Indigo, Crystal, and Psychic Kids, I talk about the phenomenon in more depth. The characteristics of this person are:

- Independent
- Assertive
- Temperamental
- Spiritually Aware
- Psychic (usually in the sect of Empathy)

The Indigo child started to be noticed around the 1970s and is believed to be the next evolution of humans those with a higher consciousness.

If you see indigo spots within the aura it can indicate a need to relieve emotional pressure. Those with indigo typically hold in their feelings until they combust. It also indicates a need for a change to bring about more of an emotional balance.

Light Blue

A COLOR of communication, light blue is the color of the peacekeeper. This person would work well in the fields of therapy and social work. They keep their emotions on ready display, and do not make any apologies for it.

Blue

A REGULAR blue indicates a balance in their emotional self; they understand themselves but temper their emotional behavior and reactions with logic and understanding. They are on a constant quest for understanding and knowledge of the world and all of its intricacies.

GREEN

Mint

THIS beautiful shade of light green, indicates that someone is going through a slight life change. It is a natural process, however, and shows that there will not be any ill effects felt from it. A smooth, healing transition.

Yellow-Green

WHEN this color shows up it means that healing for this person is going to come through communication. That they are always looking to get their ideas or issues across and they are about to be rewarded for it by getting the attention and the healing they have been looking for.

Green

LOOK for recuperation around this person; it seems that their body is trying to heal itself and it shows that there is a need to relax. I see this a lot around people who have recently had surgery or are fighting off a cold.

Dark Green

PEOPLE with a dark or hunter green see themselves as perfectly healthy and fine, however, that is merely an illusion, dark greens indicate deep emotional or physical trauma that may be buried deep down in their psyche.

Red

Pink

Pink shows a great self-love; those with pink in their aura may be considered the romantic at heart. If they are single, expect love to be coming their way and if they are not, then they share a great bond with their partner. Either way, they are in a good and stable place when it comes to their self-confidence and appreciation.

Maroon

This person is someone who has let too many things get in the way of reaching their goals. Their passion for life has faded a little. They need to look for the deeper spiritual meaning behind the scenarios that keep repeating themselves in their life.

Red

Those with red in their aura are naturally assertive and may be given to higher rates of aggression. They are natural leaders, but they need to be careful that their belief and passion do not turn into fanaticism.

Yellow

Pale Yellow

People with a pale yellow aura are pretty pleasantly natured. They have an even temperament and it suggests that they are all around in love with life. They have a nurturing ability and quite often take on the motherly role in relationships. They are highly communicative and apt to ramble when they are nervous. Although they may show a calm exterior, they have lots of energy.

Sunflower Yellow

This almost golden mustard yellow are the crème de la crème of yellows. They have a sophisticated sense of the world and more often than not end up in business. They are born diplomats with the sense of what to say and how to say it that comes to them intuitively. They have a tendency to think highly of themselves and are very protective of their privacy. Most of today's leaders will have some of this color in their aura.

Bright Yellow

These people have the gift for gab and are not afraid to use it. Much like the sun, those with a mainly a bright yellow aura have a tendency to see problems from their own perspective. "I am the center of the Universe." That does not mean they lack compassion. Oh, certainly they do, but if it does not have something to do with them, then they will not take it as seriously. People with a bright yellow aura are very good at organization and planning. They work well in roles of management and customer service.

Brown and Black

These tones can indicate issues of illness or injury that have not as of yet occurred or that are still having effects on the person often appearing like a smudge in the aura—pay close attention. I remember when I was first getting into auras and energy reading; I asked my aunt if she ever hurt her knee. She said, "No, I was a dancer and I broke my ankle and my foot quite a few times but I never hurt my knee." She did not take it as anything and went on with her day, but I could not get that visual of the brown smudge over her knee out of my head. Two days later, she tripped and fell down the stairs knocking her kneecap out of place. If you see lighter tones of brown, know that it is something coming. Darker brown means to watch closely because it is almost there, and black, well, black means it is already happening.

Gold

Look for great success around this person, financial opportunities are coming for them and they can do no wrong at this point on their path. They have reached a higher state of consciousness and really have learned to make the Universe work for them.

Silver

When you see flecks of silver, almost like little lights, there is a big change coming for this person—oftentimes in the form of a baby or a huge lifestyle change. Either way, it is a marker for Divine Inspiration and change.

Holey Auras

Why do we get holes in our aura? One theory is the aura, much like your internal energies or your chakras, record emotional and physical traumas. That is why some psychics when they look at your aura can tell where there has been pain or issues in the past, typically indicated by a brown discoloration over the area. Anything that can disrupt an electromagnetic field can mess with your aura. This includes coming into contact with certain crystals, other electronic products, people, and such. Most psychics see the holes (much like art, every psychic can sit down with a person and see something different) as black spaces, but you can actually feel them as well! Repair of the aura when it comes to holes and leaks is said to really help relieve chronic fatigue among other ailments.

To repair the aura, first you must find the holes and leaks, I will show you two methods, one by touch and the other through the use of a pendulum! It really is a fun bonding experience and it infuses some of your energy into your partner so it is just another aspect of joining together and being part of each other. (After reading the two methods of finding problem areas in the auras, instructions for fixing them follows.)

Repairing Auras Method One

1. Hold your hands on either side of your partner's head, leaving about six inches distance.

2. Start bringing them together slowly, when you feel resistance or tingling stop. You have reached the aura field.

3. Now follow that flow around the edge of the body, if you feel a draft or a dip in the energy then that is a hole.

4. Go all the way down the sides of your partner slowly then the front and back paying specific attention to the stomach, head and legs.

Repairing Auras Method Two

For this, you are going to need a pendulum. What is a pendulum? It is a stone or object hung from a string or chain. Here are some of mine.

What you did with the first method (going around all areas of the body), you will also do in the second. The best pendulum to use is one of copper as this metal is naturally attracted to electricity, however, when shopping for a pendulum, that may not be the one for you. Selecting a pendulum may take a little time and patience, but it is well worth it. They come in a variety of stones and metals. There are a few really good pendulum and crystal websites out there, but I have to say my favorite place to go pendulum shopping is Pelham-Grayson in Connecticut. You can also check your local metaphysical shop. Pendulums are fairly common and easy to find; if there isn't a place locally, then just hop on the Internet.

1. Begin by holding the pendulum about twelve inches above the Crown Chakra, hold your arm as stead as possible and let the pendulum swing. Usually it will swing parallel to the body.

2. As it swings, slowly move the pendulum forward. In this way, you can easily see when the pendulum reaches the aura, as it will seem as though it has hit a barrier and will only swing to a certain point.

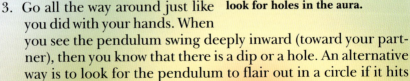

A wonderful alternative way to look for holes in the aura.

3. Go all the way around just like you did with your hands. When you see the pendulum swing deeply inward (toward your partner), then you know that there is a dip or a hole. An alternative way is to look for the pendulum to flair out in a circle if it hits a hole letting you know that energy is needed.

Filling in the Aura

All right; so now that you have found the holes, what do you do with them? Why, fill them in, of course! Much like finding the holes, there are several ways to accomplish a "fill." We look to using Universal energy to help us with this. For some, their auras may be the equivalent of a cheese grater and so we must have patience in helping them heal and it may take more than one session to do so.

Stitch Them Up

It is exactly as it sounds, you will be darning your partner's holey aura just like you would a pair of socks or trousers. Think of the aura like a cloth and your left finger like a needle. It does not have to be neat, just do a nice little saddle stitch and then smooth it over with your left palm, then continue the process around the body. Lastly, double-check your work by testing the field again with your hands or the pendulum.

Energy Fill

This is the method that I normally use, but I do not mind expending a little extra energy!

1. Place your hands on either side of the hole.

2. Then imagine a white pure light above your head (this will be similar to the chakra cleansings).

3. Bring the light down, into your body, and out your hands.

4. See the hole like a void filled with little sparks of energy; see your white energy co-mingling with the aura's sparks in the hole. Watch as those sparks get bigger and bigger, eventually filling the hole completely.

5. Go through the rest of the body.

6. Then test the aura again using your hands or the pendulum.

Strengthening Your Aura

Think of your aura as your shield: When someone steps into your "bubble," you know it. When your aura is strong, it can actually help to protect you. Alternatively, when it is weak, it can leave you feeling disconnected from yourself and completely fried. That being said, there are ways to help strengthen your aura. Most of these are pleasurable and they range from anything from a bath to crystals that you can wear that resonate with the auric field.

Cleansing Bath

>   1 lb Baking Soda
>
>   1 Cup Sea Salt
>
>   4 Tbsp Ginger Powder (optional)

Sea salt is great for cleaning wounds and removing toxins from the body, this mixture will also help to cleanse and strengthen your aura as well.

Run your bath, using warm water soak for twenty minutes.

Repeat every day for seven days and do this once every couple of months.

If you begin to be overwhelmed, depressed, or just stressed out, go ahead and begin the bathing ritual again.

Labradorite

Labradorite has been shown through Kirilian photography to heal tears in the aura. It has become known as the "stone of healers" and is often worn by nurses, body workers, and others within the health fields. A beautiful stone, it can be found in many bracelets and necklaces. The effects of holding or wearing a labradorite for twenty minutes can be maintained for a full twelve to fourteen hours.

Bubble Up

It is not as bad as it sounds I promise! You or your partner can do this exercise whenever you feel threatened. It works for both physical and spiritual protection. I use it often when I am driving for long periods, or walking home alone. I also use it if I am at a haunted location and feel threatened, or if I am around people who are just plain negative. You know the type—when you leave their house, you just feel completely drained and out of sorts.

1. Visualize yourself or your lover standing in a black space with a pinpoint of light above you or your partner.

2. Now see that light coming down around you shaped like an egg. It is God light, full of love, peace and happy feelings. It brings a feeling of warmth and tingles around your body; it is like a fog or mist.

3. Next, imagine battleship, steel going over the white light, rivets keeping it in place. (Some like to imagine the white light as a representation of the Divine Feminine, then a gold light as a representation of the Divine Masculine. You can see it in any color you like as long as it gives you that same feeling of protection.)

4. Now visualize all of the evils in the world surrounding your child and bouncing off into the universe.

It is simple to do and can be applied to anything. If you do not want negative spirits (or thieves) coming into the home do this visualization except make the bubble bigger to cover the entire house. This is a great exercise if you, your spouse, or even your children have empathic abilities and are going into large crowds so that the feelings they perceive are not so overwhelming.

A bubble of water works just as well as a bubble of light.

A variation of this is to visualize you, your lover or anyone else you are trying to protect in a suit of gold armor, that glows brilliantly and then continue on with the negative entities bouncing off of it and into the Universe.

Meridian Lines

Think of meridian lines like energy veins. They bring good Chi to all areas of the body including the organs. There are twelve major meridian lines that affect everything from the kidneys, to your eyes, to your heart. Like I said earlier in this chapter, one study was done that could not find the meridians in deceased patients. But many more have been done with live patients that have shown results. For instance, in 1950, Yoshio Nakatani demonstrated that in a specific organ disease, a number of the acupuncture points (which follow the meridian lines) actually showed less electrical resistance. In the late 1970s, Dr. Robert Becker similarly identified over fifty percent of the acupuncture points along the large intestine meridian line were of lower electrical resistance. Becker theorized that these points might be acting as semi conductors of a Direct Current system traveling along perineural cells, which wrap around each and every nerve in the body. The Direct Current became more negative as it traveled to the tips of the fingers and toes, but then it became more positive as it came back to the abdomen and the head. This easily represents the yin and yang flow that is so commonly applied to acupuncture methodology and was originally discovered over 5,000 years ago.

In 1985, Pierre de Vernejoul conducted a now famous experiment regarding the meridian lines. He actually introduced some radioactive markers called technetium 99 into the classic acupuncture points and then used a gamma camera to track the progress. From that, he was able to show how the markers actually traveled the path of the known meridian lines. They traveled quite a distance in three to four minutes around thirty centimeters. In comparison, he placed other markers willy-nilly style (but not at any acupuncture points). He also injected the markers directly into the lymphatic channels and veins, repeating the experiment and calling it his control. There was no real movement to be seen and certainly, nothing like what was shown in the meridian lines. What this showed was that meridian lines were channels, but they were just not able to be seen on any macroscopic or physical level.

Many scientists believe that it is actually collagen fibers that create the meridian lines, and that these fibers may actually have the potential to create and transmit electricity throughout our bodies. In the *Nei Ching* text it speaks of the meridian lines and how the currents only flow in one direction. Well science has helped us to

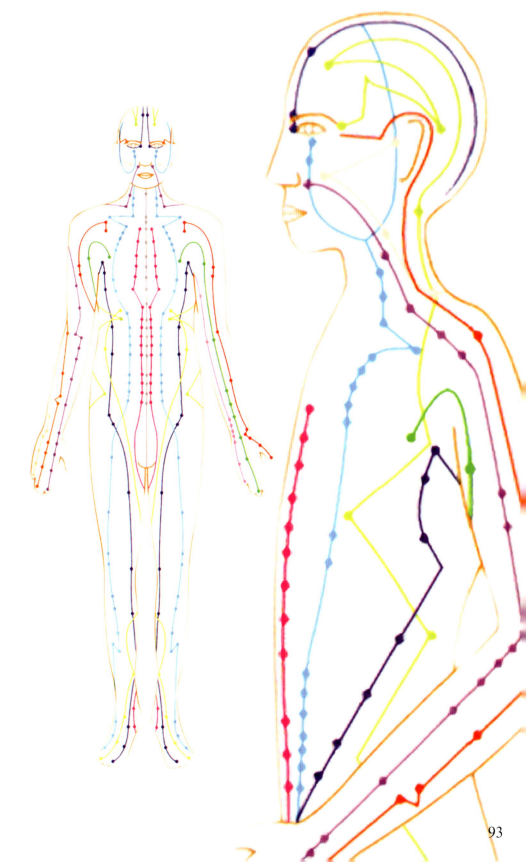

prove this to be true! These fibrous tissues only flow electrical energy in one direction—it is what they call a diode. The same direction as spoken about in the aforementioned text. Interesting, huh? So now that you know a little bit about meridian lines, let me map them out for you.

As you can see there are the twelve major meridian lines, the best way to work through these lines (other than going to an acupuncturist) is massage.

The twelve meridians each have their own function and are a continuation of that function on both sides of the body. Denise McMahon a Licensed Massage Therapist and practitioner in holistic health once told me, "What you do on one side of the body you must do on the other—it keeps things balanced." I truly believe that when it comes to dealing with these energies. Meridians, much like chakras, can get blocked or broken so that their electricity-producing qualities actually become stunted. Hence, massage and acupuncture work to stimulate these points bringing them back into alignment. What better way to play with your lover and learn their body than through massage and reflexology?

Shiatsu Massage

Shiatsu massage is renowned for its work on the meridian lines; it is a beautiful feeling to be put back into place by one of these massages. The word shiatsu literally means "finger pressure." It varies in style depending on where you are at in the world, using mainly the fingers, the heel of the hands, even legs and feet to stimulate the acupressure points along the meridian lines. But the same methodology applies; they work along the meridian lines to help stimulate the system—it is both relaxing and reenergizing.

One thing I always start with before I begin working on a client is a small prayer. It can be something simple like, "Spirits and angels, guide my hands as I help to heal, relax, and rejuvenate this person's energy and body." It does not need to be said aloud as some people do feel a little odd with my doing that, but I find that it actually relaxes my clients even more knowing that what I do is guided. Psychologically the back is the easiest place to start. When someone says "Let me massage your back." People equate it with a back rub. In addition, it is a big, solid piece of the body and it does not look like it will break easy!

How to Give a Shiatsu Back Massage

What you will need:

    Massage oil or moisturizing lotion

    A bed or massage table

    Your lover shirtless

    A couple of candles

Directions:

1. First, I suggest getting comfortable. This is going to be pleasurable for you *and* your partner. Your partner needs to be at a height where you can stand or kneel comfortably over them. Next, place one hand where the neck meets the back and the other where the spine meets the buttocks. Think of it like touching a sleeping baby, very gently; you do not want to wake the baby. Just lay your hands for approximately thirty seconds, think about how much you love your partner and want to give them pleasure when you touch them. This allows your partner's body to adjust to your touches and lets their energy know that you are doing nothing

but good. Without moving either hand begin to gently rock your partner, using the tailbone almost like a handle. The idea is to get a wave-like motion going through your partner's body so she/he melts into the floor.

2. Now is the time to bring out some massage oil or lotion. Do not put it directly on your partner but instead cup one of your hands and pour a little bit there. Depending on how big the area is that you are working on, it can vary in how much you need. You just want enough to leave a thin layer of grease that you can move around—not so much that it leaves little puddles. Rub the lotion or oil between your hands to heat it up first so that your partner does not get a shock of cold (I equate to the stethoscope at the doctors). Many professionals prefer lotion for that reason, it absorbs quickly into the skin. The best, in my opinion, is Biotone. Bring both hands up toward the top of the spine, one on either side of the spinal column, fingers pointed toward the tailbone and thumbs touching. Glide your hands down following the spine and fan them out when you reach near the base; do this four or five times. When you reach the base of the spine the last time, begin rubbing in a circular motion around the tailbone.

3. Next bring your hands all the way up to the top of the spine where the back connects with the neck. Put your thumb on either side of the spine (never on the spine); you will feel a tough muscle where the spine connects to the back muscle. Almost like a ridge, it is called the *erector spinae*. With medium pressure, follow the ridge with your thumbs all the way down the back. This should take around thirty seconds or more. If you find a hard spot or a knot, give it a little attention by letting your thumbs slowly sink deeper into it. When you feel the spot "wiggle," then become soft, you know you have released it and can move on.

4. Still at the base of the spine, stand next to your partner's side, and with both hands, reach across your partner's back slowly and with light pressure (but enough to actually lift their body for a second), go ahead and pull your hand back over to your side. Do this all the way up, then on the other side of the back, do it again.

5. Using medium pressure beginning at the base of the spine, glide your hands on either side of the spinal column all the way up the back flaring your hands out at the shoulders. Do this two or three times and be careful not to put too much pressure when directly over the spine.

6. At the top of the shoulders are the trapezius muscles. Here you are going to knead the muscles like bread. It does not need to be too hard; your thumbs should be on top of your partner's shoulders and your fingers on their back with you standing in front of their head. While doing this, continue to look for those tight spots; apply pressure (as above) to release them.

7. Have your partner lift their hand onto their back; when they do this you can easily see the shoulder blade. Run your fingers along the inner edge of the shoulder blade pressing in and down with medium pressure. You may actually feel the shoulder blade lift a little bit as the muscles release.

8. End with a few gliding strokes down the back and let your partner get up and switch. Now it is your turn.

To learn more about massage and specifically shiatsu, I suggest checking out a great video page at ehow.com. The listing can be found in the resources section of this book. The site provides information about how to stimulate each meridian and goes in depth for you. Giving massages shows how much you want to care for your lover, and the touches are a great way to start your foreplay, not to mention the benefits of stress relief. The lower back and neck are the weakest points where many people store their stress, so it is a great place to begin for anyone when giving a massage. Enjoy yourself and let your intuition guide you on what to do for your partner.

Preparing Your Space for the Psychic Sex Connection

It is so important to be prepared when you are having psychic sex; yes, it can be spontaneous, but this is a form of worship for both partners. I hear from many couples how they have sex, but it feels empty and they cannot understand why. After being in a relationship for a while with someone, you get stuck in routines! A client once told me that, "Every other Wednesday is sex night." That threw me off just a little bit. I asked her if they like to have spontaneity or how long their sex lasted, and she told me that she would love sometimes just to go after him but he had a very strict schedule that he kept to and that the sex lasted at most a half hour. Now I am a busy person myself, but I never object to a spur of the moment quickie with my hunny. However, that is not what psychic sex is about.

Psychic sex is about being present during the act of sex, joining body and energy with your lover, and showing your appreciation for all that they do. It is about reinforcing the great connection you already have and bringing relationships to new levels. It cannot be done in a half hour (at least not right away). I will admit there is a little bit of theater in this section with setting the mood and such, but you don't necessarily need it. Once you get in the psychic sex mind set, you can instill the practices anywhere you please and reap the benefits. It is just as if you were working on becoming a psychic—when you start out, you may need an aid (like tarot cards). When you begin to get comfortable and confident in your abilities and practice, you will not need anything at all.

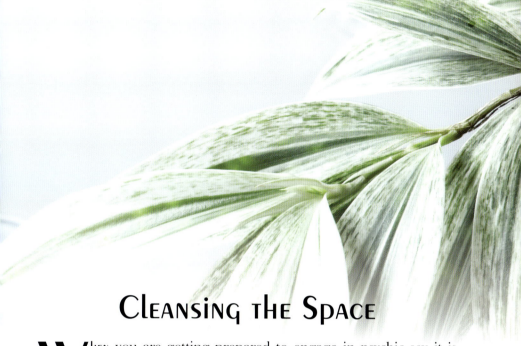

Cleansing the Space

When you are getting prepared to engage in psychic sex it is important to make sure that your space is cleansed. If there have been any stresses or issues in the home or space it can actually affect your sex experience. Granted sex is a great stress reliever in itself—it leaves your energy open to absorb negativity. Psychic sex, until you get it right, is not for everyday use. Think of it as a love ritual. Creating the right mood, means creating a fantasy. This can be easily (and cheaply) done with things you may already have lying around the home. Now that you know how to prepare yourself body, mind, and energy, let us get into preparing the space.

There are a couple different methods I am going to lay out for you here. First let's start with herbs:

White Sage

It has a long history of being used for cleansing negative spaces; some believe that it can even rid oneself and property of evil spirits. The usual use is to burn it, you can buy it dried at any local metaphysical shop or at the places listed in the resources section. If you are planning on making this an every other week or monthly ritual, then I would suggest using the places listed in the back of the book as you can get the sage in bulk. I bought one bulk bag from Azuregreen and it has lasted me over a year, that includes using it for house cleansings for clients, myself, friends and family. So you can probably figure it will last you at least twice if not three times as long!

What you will need:

    One microwavable or heat safe dish

    Lighter

    Five sage leaves or a stem

Directions:

Light the sage and put it into the dish. There will be a nice little fire for a second and then it will die down. When the smoke finally begins to waft (and believe me it will), you may want to open a window or two, as it does get thick. Sage also has the benefit of opening airways, so if you have asthma, this is a really good herb to burn. Go around your space, beginning from the North direction, counterclockwise using your hand like a fan. Get the smoke to encompass the entire room. Walk around the room three times and then place the sage on your bureau or bedside table and let it burn down.

    I love the smell of white sage and use it often, but some don't care for it as much as I do. There is an alternative, where you can still get the benefit of the sage without all of the smokiness and hassle. It is called Sage Spray. Here is how you make it:

Sage Spray

What you will need:

A small spray or perfume bottle

7 drops Sage Essential Oil

5 drops Lavender Essential Oil (optional it brings about a relaxing effect and blends nicely with the sage)

3/4 cup Water

Directions:

In your spray bottle blend water and essential oils. Screw on cover, shake and spray going in a counterclockwise direction starting in the North. Go around the room three times.

One thing that many energy workers understand is the impact of sound on the energy, both in the body and in a space. Stamping your feet or clapping your hands can help to dispel negative energies but in only works in very small areas so you will have to walk around the room, again counterclockwise.

You can also use a small bell or rattle. I like to use Tibetan singing bowls. Tap the bell three times and let the sound resonate throughout the room. Do three successions of three (in other words tap the bell nine times in three sets of three) if you are using a rattle it is similar to saging the room. Go around the room counterclockwise three times shaking the rattle to disrupt and dispel bad energy.

You must be mentally and spiritually present during any of these rituals, as it is all a matter of intent. I like to say things when I'm cleansing a home or area. I will often say things like, "I call upon the angels, to cleanse this home, the ancestors to cleanse this space aid me in my work." It just reinforces your intent.

It's Not All Candles and Roses

It's important to set a mood for loving. When you open yourself up for the Psychic Sex Connection, you will want to be in a place that is not only comfortable, but stimulates all of your senses. Really we are setting the stage for a seduction—everything from scent to color choices must be laid out so that the both of you can focus your energy purely on each other.

SCENTS

First let's start with the smell of a room, living with a man depending on their nature can sometimes be equal to living in a boys' locker room. A recent survey showed that eighty-nine percent of males believe that scent can enhance the attractiveness of women. It went on further to state that fifty-five percent would be willing to get amorous with a woman due to her scent. Even Shakespeare talked about scent in "Antony and Cleopatra."

DOMITIUS ENOBARBUS
When she first met Mark Antony, she pursed up his heart, upon the river of Cydnus.

AGRIPPA
There she appeared indeed; or my reporter devised well for her.

DOMITIUS ENOBARBUS
I will tell you. The barge she sat in, like a burnish'd throne, Burn'd on the water: the poop was beaten gold; Purple the sails, and so perfumed that The winds were love-sick with them; the oars were silver, Which to the tune flutes kept stroke, and made The water which they beat to follow faster, As amorous of their strokes. For her own person, It beggar'd all description: she did lie In her pavilion—cloth-of-gold of tissue—O'er-picturing that Venus where we see The fancy outwork nature: on each side her Stood pretty dimpled boys, like smiling Cupids, With divers-colour'd fans, whose wind did seem To glow the delicate cheeks which they did cool, And what they undid did.

AGRIPPA
O, rare for Antony!

DOMITIUS ENOBARBUS
Her gentlewomen, like the Nereides, So many

mermaids, tended her i' the eyes, And made their bends adornings: at the helm A seeming mermaid steers: the silken tackle Swell with the touches of those flower-soft hands, That rarely frame the office. From the barge A strange invisible perfume hits the sense of the adjacent wharfs. The city cast Her people out upon her; and Antony, Enthroned i' the market-place, did sit alone, Whistling to the air; which, but for vacancy, Had gone to gaze on Cleopatra too, And made a gap in nature.

AGRIPPA
Rare Egyptian!

DOMITIUS ENOBARBUS
Upon her landing, Antony sent to her, Invited her to supper: she replied, It should be better he became her guest; Which she entreated: our courteous Antony, Whom ne'er the word of 'No' woman heard speak, Being barber'd ten times o'er, goes to the feast, And for his ordinary pays his heart For what his eyes eat only.

Her perfume is what caught him first, and many men thereafter. When it comes to sexy scents and seduction, we have to stimulate our partners on all areas, so I have a list of the five best scents for sex and a few combinations that are guaranteed to intrigue. All of these scents work really well together and can be combined in any number of ways. However, don't use to many at once as it can become overpowering. These scents are also worn well by women and enhance the pheromones that women naturally give off when seeking a mate.

Neroli Essential Oil

Great for loosening those inhibitions, Neroli is well known as a scent of seduction. It is a fresh, sweet scent. The oil is derived from the blossom of the bitter orange tree (Citrus aurantium var. amara or Bigaradia).

Patchouli Essential Oil

An exotic scent that, for some, is a little overpowering on it's own, but used correctly can make you feel very empowered and magical. It heightens the senses and is very stimulating.

Rose Essential Oil

Roses remind me of old time romance; it is the Queen of the love smells.

Sandalwood Essential Oil

Think of making love in a clearing in the woods, sans the bugs, twigs, and uncomfortable rocks you may end up laying on. That is what sandalwood is all about. It has a hint of spice beneath the earthy fragrance and although woodsy, it is sweet.

Jasmine

This is my favorite among the sexy scents; it reminds you of luxury. It is not cloying and helps to boost confidence.

Other Scents

Cinnamon, black pepper and other spicy scents can be used to a degree, but you need to really be careful as the scents can easily become overpowering.

These are my favorite five. You will learn overtime, as you become familiar with blending, that there are literally thousands of scents out there to work with, each with their own properties and benefits! One of the easiest ways to make sure to get your scent into the room is with the sheets. On the last rinse put three drops of your favorite essential oil or mix. It will not overpower, but the scent will definitely be noticed.

Recipes

Spicy Lovers

What you will need:

- 2 Dram Rose Essential Oil
- 2 Dram Cinnamon Essential Oil
- A small jar with a cork or cap (if you go to the resources page, there are a couple of places that sell empty 2 dram bottles)

Directions:

In the small jar, place eight drops Rose Essential Oil and four drops Cinnamon Essential Oil.

You can also make this into a body or room spray by adding 1 Cup of water and mixing in 2 tablespoons of vodka or pure alcohol as a preservative.

Slow Seduction

What you will need:

- 2 Dram Jasmine Essential Oil
- 2 Dram Neroli Essential Oil
- A small jar with a cork or cap (if you go to the resources page there

are a couple of places that sell empty 2 dram bottles)

Directions:

In the small jar, place seven drops Jasmine Essential Oil and six drops Neroli Essential Oil. You can also make this into a body or room spray by adding 1 Cup of water and mixing in 2 tablespoons of vodka or pure alcohol as a preservative.

Earth Sex

What you will need:

2 Dram Sandalwood Essential Oil

2 Dram Patchouli Essential Oil

2 Dram Ambergris Essential Oil (optional)

A small jar with a cork or cap (if you go to the resources page there are a couple of places that sell empty 2 dram bottles)

Directions:

In the small jar, place seven drops Sandalwood Essential Oil, two drops of Patchouli essential oil and four drops Ambergris Essential Oil. You can also make this into a body or room spray by adding 1 Cup of water and mixing in 2 tablespoons of vodka or pure alcohol as a preservative.

These are just three out of a huge number of combinations you can make; it is all a matter of taste. I love to blend oils when I can and doing so on an intuitive level is great. Just be sure to study the oils and their benefits and what the recommended amounts are. As some may have side effects if you use too much. For example, Clary Sage is a great seduction scent but only in small doses as it is also used as a sedative and can inhibit the sex drive.

Colors

Next, it is time to move on to colors, now mind you I am not saying that you have to have absolutely everything; these are merely suggestions. You go with what you love and your idea of romance is. Colors have meaning, and so we must look at what your intention is for this bout of lovemaking, do you want to manifest a career opportunity for yourself, do you want to feel as one with your lover, do you want to reach a new spiritual level? Depending on your intent, the colors you pick need to be a conscious choice, as they will facilitate that need. You don't need to go painting the walls but laying on these colors (bed sheets, pillows, rugs) or wearing them will help.

An artist's color wheel is very helpful when it comes to selecting which combination of colors you would like to use based on your intent.

White

Can be used for anything, because it is all colors! White represents purity and cleansing, wholeness and completion. It can help to overcome obstacles and help with new beginnings.

Black

This is the absence of all color, and the color of the Void from which life's mysteries emerge. It is a great protective color and one that stands for resilience.

Gray

Is a good color to incorporate if you are blending multiple colors and want one to have less of an effect than another. So say you want to use blue during your sexual experience in order to open better communication pathways between yourself and your lover. Nevertheless, you do not want things to become too heavy in that department; you just want to talk a little more. Than you would get blue bed sheets and mix them with some gray pillow shams. Gray is a neutral in any of its shades and can be mixed with any color that you would like to bring the intensity down on.

Green

If you feel a need for change or growth on any level (money, career, spiritually, mentally or physically), it also brings balance to the energy in the relationship.

Blue

Opens the flow of communication, allowing freedom of expression and movement. It can also bring peace to an otherwise chaotic situation and helps relieve stress. Use it to help stimulate energy flow if you feel there are blocks in the relationship. Blue is also known for its healing qualities.

Purple

A combination of red and blue, the warmest and coolest colors, purple has long been associated with magic and mysteries, royalty adorned themselves with this color. It is a color of purpose. With the influence from red lending focus and blue's freedom of thought, purple is a color of inspiration and imagination. It is great for those who suffer from depression, for couples who are trying to move forward in their lives and take the next step. Whether it be buying a house or getting married, if obstacles are in the way, then purple will help to give the divine inspiration to move forward with them.

Indigo

This color will help you connect with yourself and blend energies with your partner. Also it is a great color for helping solve problems between two people.

Red

This color brings confidence, if you are nervous about taking a risk or making a blind leap of faith red is the color to have. Not only is it known as a color of love but it brings action to the scene, if you do not know what to do or where to go in your relationship this is a great color to help you figure it out. This is also a color of fertility and will aid those who are looking to become pregnant. This is also an awesome color to have around if you are looking to seal a deal or make negotiations.

Orange

This is a success color, if you are looking to start a new venture, hoping for a promotion or looking to seal a deal this is the color to use.

Yellow

This color brings clarity and awareness. Depending on your intention, you may want some divine clarity on a certain subject; this can help. It also brings money and fortune, so if you have been looking for a pay raise or increase in business this is the color for you.

Candles are an important part of any romantic scene, but you don't need them. Soft lighting will do just fine. One of my favorite ways to arrange soft light is to get mesh cloth in whichever color stimulates my intent and to place it over my lamp. That way the whole room glows in the color. If you are intent on using candles, you can actually dress them in an oil that you like. Whether you use votives or tapers, this method can be applied, it will also charge your candles with your intent. If you do not want them to smell, you can simply use vegetable oil.

Take the candle in your left hand dip the finger and thumb of your right into the oil. Focusing on your intent draw the fingers of your right hand from the middle of the candle up and then from the middle of the candle down. This seals your intent within the candle. Use the color choices guide above to pick your colors for your intent.

SET YOUR INTENTIONS

WE talked a little earlier about setting a mood and setting intentions. I will not expand on that subject. The whole inspiration for this book was an article I wrote a year or so ago called, "Success Through Orgasm" for carrieanddanielle.com. In it I outlined a whole guide to manifesting your desires through sex. That article became one of the most viewed on the website, and soon clients and even strangers were asking me about it!

Now is the time to get conscious about what you would like to see accomplished. Talk amongst the both of you as to what you would like to set your intention to be. Success in career, fertility, a new home, more money, a change in job, peace to the world—there are no limits. Whatever it is, it must be a completely cohesive image. I would suggest listing everything out and agreeing to it; that way you both know for sure you will be thinking about the same things.

Now it is time to create an image. This is something for the both of you to focus on while have your psychic sex experience. Take a piece of paper and a pencil; both you and your partner draw whatever your intention is. If you are not the best at drawing, don't worry about it. You can also write around the image, don't worry if you feel

it's too messy or it looks like a bunch of stick figures. As long as you both know what it means, that is all that matters. I would also suggest investing in some colored pencils! Remember colors carry their own energy and now that you know what those colors mean, you can easily incorporate them into your design.

Say I wanted to bring emotional balance to myself, because I work with the Tarot, so many Cups have always symbolized emotions. Therefore, I may do something as simple as putting three Cups in a straight line. Or if I wanted a new house I would go ahead and draw out what I would like for that house to look like. I would not put limits on where it is; by sending out the energy, you are asking Universe to set it all up for you, which it will. If I were looking for a better job, or one for my hunny, I would draw a picture of a check with a really nice sized annual, weekly, or monthly salary. I would not put the company's name on it, because it may be that you or your partner has to go through a job change to get the better paycheck. There are a few things you want to leave open ended, mainly the how and why, but you can put goals on there as well. Just be aware that in the midst of passion it is difficult to think and let yourself succumb; you either sacrifice one or the other so the easier the image to focus on the better.

Another easy way to create the picture is by using images on the internet, although anything you can do to put both of your energies into it is best. Choosing pictures, words, and fonts that resonate with you and your lover also work. Here is one my lover and I made.

Notice the simplicity, simply an open door and the Empress Tarot card. Nothing special, with a couple of words, creativity and new opportunities; little did we know how much of an impact that one picture would have on us later on. Not even three days after having utilized this picture, I was asked to fill in for another psychic on a ghost hunt. I got a call from a production company for a new series they were shooting and then my spouse got a couple of new job opportunities. It was exactly as we had envisioned and with the span of time we had been tossing around and decided to focus on.

Everything is open to us; it is a matter of reaching out and going for it. Sex is merely one way to do this. Alternatively, you could take this concept and create a dream board. This is a great project to do with your lover whether working on one board together or working on two separate projects it can be a fun bonding experience.

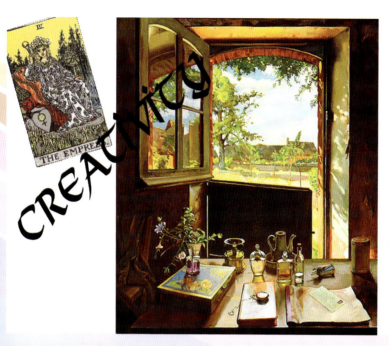

Dream Board

What is Needed:

Magazines	Scissors	Tacks
Pen	Markers	
Stickers	Glue	

Poster board
(Usually, I stick with white, but go with a color you are drawn to)

Computer
(In case the magazines don't have the words or pictures you want)

Newspaper
(To lay down so you don't get everything all messy)

Dream Board Directions:

Take your newspaper and lay it out on the floor or table then put the poster board in front of you. Go through the magazines, the internet and everywhere else. Try to find everything you ever wished for no matter how abstract the image, if it is a happy loving family then get a parenting magazine and cut out the picture. A slim sexier you, then get a fitness magazine, make sure to incorporate key words of success.

I CAN   EMPOWER   FAITH   SUCCESS   (*like you didn't see that coming*)

If you are looking for more money or a house then cut out pictures that signify those things. The point is for you to pour every want and wish onto that board. It is to be a culmination of all of your life's dreams at this moment.

Later your dreams may change at which point you can make a new board for yourself. As you plaster your pieces onto the board infuse them with your energy be conscious of your wishes and visualize them happening. Not necessarily the how (leave that part to the creative energies) but the feeling of it having already happened. If you are strapped for cash and want to be able to pay bills, summon up that wonderful feeling of accomplishment after the mortgage is paid and still having funds left over. If you need a new cell phone, see yourself driving or walking down the street talking on it. Doing this affirms to Universe that you believe it WILL happen no *if's ands or buts'* about it.

When you have finished putting the board together put it in a place you will see it often. Mine is my home office where I spend a lot of time answering e-mails, taking phone calls, etc. It has both my personal and business goals on it. So far I've reached most of them. I wanted to write for a living. I am, thanks to a "fluke." When I picked up a regional ghost book and realized my group was mentioned, I got in touch with the publisher and we had a contract the next day. After that I went on to write other books through this company and was accepted as a freelance writer for a few blog sites.

Take five minutes out of every day to sit with the board, look at it, and bring back those feelings surrounding the things you want or need. Visualize yourself having them, focus on what it feels like, and be there in that moment in your mind. Do not allow doubt to come into play here, there is no doubt, only your will. I suggest keeping the board for a span of three months or more.

Alternative

If you do not want anything to permanent on the board, you can always opt to go with a corkboard. An investment in one small corkboard and some tacks can do a world of good as that way you can switch out the pictures and phrases whenever you please.

How To Have A Psychic Sex Experience

"Nor can I say 'I love you,' when I have ceased to be, and you have ceased to be: we are both caught up and transcended into a new oneness where everything is silent, because there is nothing to answer, all is perfect and at one. Speech travels between the separate parts. But in the perfect One there is perfect silence of bliss."

~*D. H. Lawrence*
Women in Love, Chapter 27

All right, so now that we have gone through all of the lessons, let's get to the fun stuff. The sex itself! There are a couple of things to discuss first. Energy is a cool living thing, something that we can utilize in our daily lives, manipulate and harness. Balance in energy can be maintained in any relationship heterosexual or homosexual it does not matter. So many people believe that balance is obtained by two polarities, and essentially this is true, however when it comes to energy, it does not matter. Of course, the energy exchange is a little different, for a male-male couple we must understand that both harness the energy of the God-form the aggressor, the energy that really helps to push things along. So we must respect that it may be more difficult (unless one in the couple has more feminine leanings) to really find true emotional balance. The same goes with female-female couples where the energy is more nurturing and spiritual, you may find it more difficult (again unless one has the more aggressive traits inherently considered to be part of the male God-form) to materialize things, but emotional balance and nurturing of any type would be easily created through the energy exchanges. Some of us may want to keep these things to ourselves and prefer to use this guide on their own. Does masturbation work in psychic sex? Yes, yes it does. Granted things may not come as quickly as you would like because there is a single energy being sent out there not two, however, energy is energy and any form is acceptable.

Before we get into foreplay, I would like to talk to you about touch. Rubbing, massaging, caressing all evoke different feelings and emotions. It is important when incorporating psychic sex that you think of what emotions you wish to impart to your partner. When going around the different chakra points there are certain touches that will create a higher response. I will list them out for you here:

Root

Women: Small circular rubbing motions using usually three fingers applying medium pressure helps to awaken the Root Chakra.

Men: Wide, light, back and forth motions around the Root Chakra area, not touching the penis, the vibrations caused by the back and forth motion helps to awaken his Root Chakra.

Sacral

Women: Light caresses in one direction (usually left) around the sacral gives enough of a vibration to awaken the energy.

Men: Have palms meet in the center of the chakra and caress outward and around sides.

Solar

Women: Much like men's Sacral, grasp your lover so that your palms lay flat over her belly button thumbs meeting and pointing towards her head. With a slight pressure move, your hands up towards the rib cage in a gliding motion until you reach the base of the rib cage then gently fan them out.

Men: Using both hands do long downward gliding strokes from the top of the sternum down to the navel. Repeat three or four times to really get the chakra open.

Heart

> **Women:** Using your palm with barely any pressure, rub in a clockwise circular motion in the valley between the breasts.

> **Men:** Place your palms over the pectoral muscles so that the thumbs cross over the Heart Chakra apply medium pressure down and away from you in time with your breathing. Do this three times.

Throat

Women: Grabbing the throat lightly so thumbs rest over the Throat Chakra, fan your thumbs back and forth towards your palms, then back towards the Throat Chakra.

Men: Lightly grasp the skin of the throat with your thumb and forefinger, roll it between your thumb and forefinger applying no pressure at all.

Third Eye

Women: Lightly massage the center of the forehead using and up and down motion with two fingers.

Men: Lightly massage the center of the forehead using two fingers in a circular motion from the right side of the forehead to the left and back again. Repeat this twice.

Crown

Women: Beginning at the top of head run fingers through hair almost like pulling it back into a ponytail using nails to lightly rake the scalp.

Men: Beginning at temples place hands on either side and making a medium-sized circular motion caress the scalp.

At the same time as you are using your hands to help open the chakras to receiving your energy, you are also sensitizing your lover's body. This will help to create a more intense experience for the both of you and should be included in any foreplay.

The Art of Foreplay

The worst torture and the greatest pleasure, foreplay can instantly heighten a sexual experience, but it goes beyond just the bedroom. On more than one occasion, I have made a point of teasing my lover throughout the day, whispering things in their ear, letting them know how much I want them. Only to move away before they can catch me. By the time that we actually got to bed, we were so hot for each other there was no heavy petting required.

Foreplay is seduction. It should be tempered and cool, with the underlying promise of the pleasure to come. It serves a dual purpose. Firstly, it feels good and you are not yet the mindless creature that most of us turn into when we are actually in the midst of a good tumble, so you can take the time to enjoy and process the experience. On the flip side, the older you get the harder it may become to be ready at a moment's notice, so foreplay helps to build you both up. Women in particular need prolonged stimulation in order to have a truly gratifying orgasm. There is an art to foreplay, men, the one piece of advice I will give you is not to rush to the genitals. Women, be confident in your body, no matter what, and express yourself to your fullest. The sounds of your own moans and groans not only turn your partner on but you as well.

Teasing Throughout The Day

If you are a couple, it's the little things that you can do throughout the day that lets your lover know exactly what you are thinking about.

Men

When your woman is getting dressed and she is in her bra, pull down one of her bra straps and kiss that area lightly then pull it back up. Simple, but effective. You can do the same thing with the underwear and get your point across. If she wants sex there and then, don't give in no matter how tempting. Confidence is key; showing your confidence to your woman is a total turn on. It goes back to the caveman days when men hunted and were warriors, the most seasoned and accomplished would have their pick of women. Unfortunately, in that respect, times have not changed much.

Pay attention gentlemen, it is the little touches that please a woman.

WOMEN

EVER communicative creatures, you must realize that only six percent of what you say actually matters; the rest is body language and the tone of your voice. There is no need to be overtly sexual; it does not take much to get the point across. However, when at a crowded party, if you decide to "send a message," feel free to whisper in your mate's ear that you are not wearing any underwear, see how fast they leave the party. Taking care of your partner is one of the quickest ways to turn them on, little touches throughout the day, a soft pat or rub on the back, touch of the hand, sends many signals. Your eyes and body need to become your tools for teasing your lover.

Divine Foreplay

When you first come to each other to attain the psychic sex experience, your chakras and energies should be in alignmen. Some couples decide to incorporate it into their foreplay; the massages and spiritual healings are a way of showing love and receiving love. That alone can be a turn on. I often find many couples forget that they are from the divine, Gods and Goddesses from different pantheons; each of us is a deity in our own right. It is a beautiful thing to release that wild vibrant God or Goddess upon your partner, to find that inner being and release it.

For women, the Goddess symbol often is seen as a "mother to the world" type, but She is also an extremely sensual creature. Look at Bastet the Cat Goddess, long and lean, She is a Goddess of fertility, sexuality, and birth. She is beautiful, She is graceful, and She is demanding of her lovers. Or look at Freya, a Norse Goddess; She represents the warrior woman, proud and strong, capable of anything and yet She is a wonderful lover who is easy to catch but hard to keep, mysterious and alluring. We each own every aspect of every Goddess out there. It is time to let Her out.

For men, the God symbol often is seen as "the Father of All." Granted, He is that, but He is also a gifted lover whose dark nature entices many women. Look at Pan, God of the Wild Wood, with a long engorged penis; He pleased many women, and through His loving, nurtured their spirit. A beautiful man-beast, He represents the God aspect in each of you, that essential self that drives you to mate, please your partner, and pro-create. That beautiful part of yourself that pushes you to do better, be better and know better, to succeed no matter what. You each own every aspect of every God out there. It is time to let Him out.

Imagine yourself to be a deity, who would you choose? Juno? Artemis? Lugh? Odin? I am not asking you to adopt their name, merely their power. Seeing yourself as this deity will help you to feel empowered to feel emblazoned with their mysticism; essentially it invokes that deity to you. Allow yourself to absorb this deity into yourself, their confidence flows through you, their will is meant to be carried out, whatever your focus is for manifestation will happen because it is your WILL.

As you invoke your Goddess or God persona, and feel their power, come into your body, run your hands along your lover. From the top of their scalp down to their toes, as your hands run over their body, see

Ancient Babylonian figure dating from between 1792 and 1750 BC of Queen of the Night, probably a goddess of sexual love.

A Greek Goddess tempts a Greek God,

them leave faint traces of a silver (for her) or gold (for him) energy. This is your divine essence, that part of you that is your Goddess or God, see that essence seep into their pores, mixing with their own energy. Take this opportunity to explore your partner, each facet of their body, discover what tickles them, what makes them moan, find it all. Wherever you touch, lick, kiss, or bite leaves some trace of that divine energy. As you continue to take the lead in this seduction, your energy will begin to meld even deeper with that of your partner. See your hands glow that beautiful silver, and sink into your lover's energy. See your chakra points aligning with theirs, threads of your mixed energy cocooning you as you tease your lover.

The point of this exercise is to not focus on the genitals but the whole of your lover and their energy. If you feel that your lover has reached a point, where they may be overly excited stop for a minute or two and let the energy wane, then go back in and build it up again. Give each other this treatment, building up the energy and then letting it go back down. As you, do this, it actually will facilitate an aura expansion and cause your energy to connect on a deeper and deeper level. The threads of your energy will combine, creating almost like a cloth that connects the two of you, a blanket of your energy that will encase you as you move forward through the psychic sex experience.

Energy Foreplay

Instead of focusing on empowering yourself as a divine figure, we are going to focus on simply your energy body. You and your partner both choose a color; this color will represent your energy body. Let your partner know which color you wish to be. Visualize yourself and your lover in your respective colors, and have them do the same. Sit on the bed or floor facing each other and hold hands interlocking your fingers palms touching. Hold your hands in between your bodies. Instead of going straight to touching and petting visualize your energy seeping through your hands into your lovers, carry that energy up and through until the colors become mixed, have your lover do the same. See your Heart Chakras pulsate and swirl the lights reach out and touch. See your Crown Chakras do the same, now your beautiful Indigo Chakra which represents your psychic self. As your Indigo Chakra connects with your lover's, you can suddenly see through their

eyes. Feel their feelings and understand their thoughts. You move forward with the exercise, joining the Throat Chakra then sacral and Solar Chakras, finally ending with Root Chakra. These slight threads thicken as you continue to experience what your lover feels and vice versa.

Suddenly, the threads grow taunt and they begin to pull you both together, closer, your hands release, and sitting, you begin to explore each other with your hands. Through the energy body, you can feel not only your pleasure but your lover's as well; their touch is your touch. Do not kiss or fondle merely caress each other, do not break eye contact, continue to caress each other. Slowly the strings pull you together, as your lover caresses you and you caress your lover—it is overwhelmingly pleasurable. Through this blending of the energy bodies you see your auras expand cocooning you both, joining and celebrating by flaring brilliant colors as you love on each other. If the pleasure becomes too overwhelming, stop for a moment and continue to look each other in the eyes. When it dies down, go back to the caressing again. You should pass by the genitals, you may caress around them but do not touch them. The foreplay should last for between twenty or thirty minutes, if you are enjoying yourself, feel free to go on for as long as you like. I had one set of clients who enjoyed the blending of their energy so much that they did it all of the time, even if they didn't complete the sexual act; it made them feel so deeply interconnected and it would last throughout the night and day. It is a great exercise for reconnecting with your partner after you have been emotional or physically apart for an extended period.

Going After Your Pleasure

Our body language says an awful lot, but when we are in bed and in the heat of the moment, whether our lover comes to fruition too rapidly or is not hitting all of the right places, we can miss a lot. Therefore, to get both what you want and make your lover more confident in bed, communication is essential. You do not need to tell your lover that they are "doing it wrong." Simply tell them what you do like, have an open conversation about. A way to do it, without feeling so much embarrassment is to lay their hand or move their head where you want them to go. Finally, another way to show them how you like to be touched is to masturbate in front of each other, make it a sharing experience.

How To Orgasm

When it comes time for your orgasm, that is when you need to bring your picture and intent to the forefront. But it is important that you do not rush to the finish line. Thirty percent of men reach the point of ejaculation sooner than they would like, in the 1940s, Alfred Kinsey did a study on male sexuality including everything from heterosexuality to homosexuality. He found that seventy-five percent of men, at that time, ejaculated within two minutes of entering the vagina. Now I know for women, this can be very disheartening, but worry not! Tantra will help us to solve this problem; it is the celebration of life through sex; it is a sacred sex that connects us to the Universe.

No one would believe that in order to control ejaculation (on both sides) that you need to be in a state of constant awareness so you can stop and start again, but that is not necessarily true. We see the big "O" as the epitome of pleasure. If you have sex it is so that you can orgasm; your muscles will contract and give you that ten seconds of ecstasy. Right? Then afterwards you have a messy clean up, but that is the price to pay for good sex is it not? No, not really. In practicing Tantra, the point is to not concentrate on the orgasm, but the pleasure itself, do not focus on the release, but what you feel in the moment. Relax yourself. Tantric sex is much slower and so it is less intense, but more deeply felt by both partners. Check in with yourself to find where your level of arousal is. This will tell you if you need to slow down when you are getting close to the point of release. Keep focus on the pleasure, not the destination and you will be more apt to pace yourself, take your time to savor each new stimulus. It is about absorbing all the pleasure you can take, when you do feel the orgasm coming on, it is imperative that you work the energy away from your genitals. You will have an inner orgasm.

Avoiding The Physical Orgasms

In this practice, you're going to use sexual breathing to spread your excitement away from your hot zone. The whole point is to learn to absorb the orgasmic energy and use it to facilitate positive change and manifestation. But first we must bring to you the point where you can bear intense amounts of stimulus with the least reaction.

1. Find a comfortable sitting position for both you and your partner.

2. Decide who is going to go first. At this point we will assume it is the male who is going to first try this practice of relaxing and breathing. Your breath is going to be vital to your orgasm control. Ask your partner to begin stroking your penis and scrotum slowly; it is up to you to tell them how you would like it done (if you want lubrication or not).

3. While being given pleasure, focus on your breath—inhale slowly into your Sacral Chakra. It is okay to motion with your hips, undulate your body, and show your pleasure. Rock your sexual energy all the way up your body.

4. Slowly have your partner accelerate their stimulation when you reach a medium level of excitement, stop for a second, and let it calm down. Do this three times.

5. Next have your partner continue stimulation, except when you get to the same medium level excitement, have them slow down their play but not stop altogether. Focus on your breath, open your eyes wide, inhale through the nose deep into your sacral (belly) and hold your breath for a count of six.

6. Exhale for a count of five. As you do, visualize a stream of bright red-orange energy shooting from your penis; inhale again through the nose, see that same energy move up from your groin, thrust your pelvis a couple of times to help shift the energy upward.

7. Your medium level excitement should slow to a lower level. Can you feel it just using the breathing techniques? Keep going with the exercise until you can. See how long you can keep at a medium peak level while adjusting your breathing. Eventually you may become desensitized to your partner's play. That is where areas such as the perineum can be extremely helpful. Be specific to your partner as to exactly how to change stimulus to bring you to a medium or high level of intensity. If it becomes too much and you feel like you are going to have a physical orgasm, have your partner stop. Bring the excess energy back up through the groin and continue when the intensity subsides.

8. Keep going with this exercise. The first time you try it, shoot for three times at medium level intensity, the next time, five. Then up it to high intensity for three. You do not have to do it all at once; try it over the span of a month, spreading

Masturbating in order to help your lover is a great way to get him/her to understand how you like to be touched.

out the sessions as you wish. However, do not work with this method any less than twice a week. In order for you to build up tolerance and have this practice become second nature, you must work with it frequently.

9. As you practice and work your way closer to release, see if you can stave off your arousal level just by controlling your breath, breathing slower and deeper, without your partner changing anything. When you can reach that precipice, just about to fall off the cliff, and holding on with your last three fingers, you are bound to experience an implosive orgasm. Where you will feel your energy literally vibrates like a tuning fork. Hold on to that energy and push it outward through your Crown Chakra and send your intent with it. This is the point where many claim to actually have visions and see the future. Aleister Crowley was really into this back in his day and would have several aides help him in his ritual.

10. Now reverse roles and begin to help your partner achieve that same level of satisfaction and spiritual connection. Really pay attention to their instructions on how to touch them and where they are most sensitive, do not go too fast too quickly, and above all, be patient.

What is great about these exercises and the Tantric practice? After these internal orgasms, you lose little if no energy and can go on with your practice for hours! During these sessions, it is very normal to have an actual spiritual experience. They call the end result "bliss" for a reason. You will feel an ultimate connection with the Divine energy and feel the oneness with Universe as a whole. While you and your partner go through the exercise above, have them focus on your intent. This is so that when they do orgasm, the energy that shoots out will carry the intent with it and into the Universe. That is the basis for psychic sex; just because we talk of orgasm, it does not necessarily mean the *messy* type. This practice can actually cause your lover to have multiple orgasms, and extend the pleasure for both of you. Just remember to be aware of how your are feeling.

During this exercise whoever is play the supporting role should also be focused on the intent, as you stimulate your partner, envision your energies combining your intents mixing; this may also bring you to the height of passion as you feel what they feel.

Psychic Sex Positions

"The only unnatural sex act is that which you cannot perform."

~ Prof. Alfred Kinsey

There are hundreds of different positions that one can use during sex the best ones are the ones that hit as many of the erogenous zones as possible and that keep as many chakras aligned as possible. I am going with the most common positions and how to manipulate them to benefit our needs. Many of us were taught the "sex is a sin" concept—I know I was. My mother scared me so bad I didn't have my first kiss till I was fifteen because I was so afraid. Nevertheless, in order for psychic sex to work, we need to shift our consciousness from "sex is sin" to sexuality is the way to our soul. Our path to learning, healing, and understanding, it is a way of self-discovery when the energies present themselves in our partners and ourselves.

In Tantra, the point of sex between two lovers is to raise the kundalini energy, often depicted as a snake that follows the spine—it is a beautiful energy system. The point of Tantric sex is not to "pound away" at your partner, but to simply relax, with slow grinding movements that help to build the energy between you. Be constantly aware of your partner's energy.

The standard missionary is one of my favorites for psychic sex as it keeps eye contact and has the added benefit of keeping the chakras aligned. However, do not think that it has to be boring; with a little creativity, you can turn a Puritan-style romp into a hot and heavy psychic sex session. Whisper in your lover's ear what you want to do, or how much you love what they are doing. Have the woman splay her legs out as far as possible thus giving the male perfect access. This way his groin will be in direct contact with her vagina. Another way to do this is to have the male place one of her legs on his shoulder or even both, each will give him a greater chance of hitting her "G-spot."

Doggy-style is a great psychic sex position, but not in the raunchy porno way. Have the woman get on all fours, and the man mounts her from behind and then leans over so that the male's chest is against

Some of the most common sex positions.

her back. This also allows the male the freedom to play with her clitoris. Women love to be cuddled and stimulated and although many term this to be a "porno" position, having the male lean over in this way gives some great intimacy and keeps the chakras connected and in alignment. One way to flow right into another position is to lift her upper body so that you are both on your knees. You can then go right into a reversal of the frog posture described by Sheikh Nefzawi in *The Perfumed Garden* where you lay her down on her stomach with her legs splayed as far apart as possible. Closing the woman's legs the man and woman can intertwine their arms and enjoy the feelings of being fulfilled.

The Mortar and Pestle is one of my absolute favorites. Have the man sit, legs splayed, then the woman comes and sits in his lap facing him with her legs splayed in the opposite direction (behind him). The point is not to ride him but instead to simply sit, this allows a great openness in the Heart Chakra. It also allows to both caress and play with each other's bodies. When you finally cannot take it anymore, lift the woman up a little bit, and have the woman move her hips in a circular motion on the way down.

I definitely do not expect things to stay confined to the bedroom, some of the best positions for a woman are those that she can control. Have the man sit on the couch, she should straddle him so that she can use her hands to brace herself on the back of the couch. This gives her enough support to ride the man to orgasm. She could even just keep one hand on the back of the couch so that she is free to play with her clitoris. This can also be done in a chair. Some women find this position easier on the couch or in a chair because their legs may not be long enough to sustain them when straddling her partner on a flat surface. There is another alternative that I have found very useful in these situations. Have the woman face opposite her lover so that he has a nice view of her buttocks. This is an extremely sensuous pose and allows the woman full control.

There is one beautiful variation to the above position which is to have the man lay on the floor or bed, legs out in a "V" shape and have the woman straddle the man; her legs should scissor around his body. Now both the man and the woman relax into a reclining position, and enjoy the feeling of being one with each other in this moment. In this position, the woman cannot ride the man but grinding and playing with the partner's body is an extremely pleasurable experience.

Two spoons is an absolutely great position. It allows for great stimulation for both partners; have the woman lay on her side, the man lays next to her so his chest is to her back. Have her lift her top leg over her partner's so that she is open to him. Let him enter her, the man is almost guaranteed to hit her G-spot. The reason for this is because women, much like other animals, are built to be entered from behind so it easier to get the woman to find release because of this.

This is just a start, be creative and have no fear! I have included a list of recommended reading to further your sexual education. There are so many positions out there and each are gratifying in their own right, I would suggest getting a couple of the books on the reading list, playing hooky from work and spending a day trying some that you make up. The best things are led by your intuition; do what feels right and let the sex progress naturally.

The After-Sex Connection

After the psychic sex experience, it is important that you both cleanse your bodies. Oftentimes we view sex as a release of stress and sometimes-negative emotions. The process of cleansing the body is as much a symbolic one as it is a hygienic one. Thinking of cleaning up such a mess is not always a pleasurable thought. However, there was always one practice from *The Perfumed Garden* that I absolutely loved. Get two wash cloths and a bowl of medium-hot water. If you would like, feel free to add a little essential oil to the water; I prefer tea tree essential oil when ending a session, as I find its astringent qualities useful (it is commonly used to treat vaginal infections and is safe to use on the genitals) and the smell refreshing and invigorating. Simply add four drops to every one and a half cups of water. That is plenty for this purpose. The other benefit is that the smell is androgynous, so the man will not go around smelling like a flower and the female like an earthy lumberjack.

Have the man wash the woman first, he will be sure to make it sensual, wash her labia, all around her clitoris, wash just inside the inner thigh. This is more than just an act of cleanliness it serves multiple purposes. By applying the heat it will actually help with possible irritation she may feel later on, it honors her and shows the man's appreciation for having her as his sex partner, also it is an act of complete love.

Next, the woman will get up and serve her lover in the same fashion, being sure to clean the head of his penis and underneath his scrotum, as well as the thighs. She should take her time and make it as sensual an experience as possible.

Increase in Psychic Connection

When you go through the psychic sex experience, there are bound to be some energetic changes that will occur; these changes will not necessarily happen right off the bat, but over time. Many of my clients express marked changes around three or four months after starting to use the techniques contained within the book—one of which is of course the increase in psychic ability between you and your partner.

There are many games that you can play to further your psychic abilities. This helps in making you more susceptible to the energies during psychic sex and giving you an even deeper connection.

Push

This game is great, especially where you are beginning to get comfortable with the feeling of energy and manipulation. This will do nothing but help you to sharpen your energy channeling skills. It is all about sending the energy into your partner. Sit facing one another. Have your partner lay their hands palm up; you hold yours a half inch above their palms facing down. Imagine a color energy for yourself—pink, purple, black, red; it does not matter. Have your lover do the same. Share the colors you have chosen. Now close your eyes and visualize yourself filled with that color, and your lover filled with their chosen color. Almost like a thermometer, you are going to try to fill your lover with your energy and your lover will try to push back and move their energy to your body.

Couples that I have taught this to have been surprised; the figure it is just creative visualization. But then when they actually try to play the game, they find resistance for some reason. They get to the wrists and no matter how hard they push, the color won't go any farther, or at the elbows, same thing. The point is to be the first to fill your lover up to the shoulders.

The more you play the game, the easier it will become to detect when you lover is pushing their energy towards you. Some get tingles in the arms, others heat. Either way, you will know when the invasion is occurring.

What Am I Thinking?

This is a great game to work on your telepathy skills with your partner. One of you will play the "receiver," the other will be the "sender." Get two pens and two pieces of paper, one each for you and your lover. Have the sender pick one of three shapes either square, triangle, or circle. The receiver's job is to psychically sense the shape that the sender is thinking of. As the sender, their duty is to scream the shape as loudly as possible in their mind. Do not be discouraged if it does not work the first few times—as with any muscle, the psychic mind needs practice.

Just these two games combined with all of the exercises in this book are plenty to get you started.

Fertility

"A grand adventure is about to begin."
~ *Winnie the Pooh*

Winnie the Pooh is more than just a fictional children's character to me; he is the western version of Buddha. A blank slate as it were; one thing that I constantly get asked is about fertility and whenever I am asked I always go back to Winnie the Pooh simply for this reason. If only there were a big button you could push that would make you pregnant in an instant—guaranteed. When we cannot have something, we want it even more. We stress about it, obsess about it, and get depressed about it. I am not saying this is the case for every couple with fertility issues as many do have physical issues. Nevertheless, I find more often than not that stress is a huge factor in conception for those who come to my table. A write up was done recently in *Slate Magazine* about the effects of stress and infertility. It finally seems like some the doctors may be making some headway in this area.

Scientists have suspected for decades that depression might play a role in infertility, but the connection has been understudied and hard to establish. For starters, plenty of depressed women have no problem getting pregnant, and many infertile women feel fine. And although some 40 percent to 50 percent of infertility cases are unexplained, the majority have a physical cause. A mind-body program won't fix blocked fallopian tubes or rehabilitate old eggs. In fact, several studies have shown that a woman's psychological well-being has little effect on IVF outcomes.

But mental health specialists are increasingly recognizing that a subgroup of depressed women may also have trouble conceiving. It makes sense from an evolutionary perspective, explained Domar, an assistant professor of obstetrics, gynecology, and reproductive biology at Harvard Medical School. A severely depressed woman might have trouble taking care of herself and wouldn't be in good shape to deal with the demands of a new baby. Another theory holds that depression increases the levels of the stress hormone cortisol, which leads to higher blood pressure, blood sugar, and the likelihood of getting sick. Researchers have speculated that cortisol might affect fertility but don't know how. Perhaps the hormone changes the timing of ovulation, when the egg is released for fertilization, or messes with pregnancy hormones, or prevents embryos from implanting into the uterine lining. No one knows.

When you do have a physical cause for your infertility, it can feel like a barren wasteland. Some women go straight to defeatist attitudes and say, "It wasn't meant to be" or "I feel old and dried up." Others lose face and hope. A small percentage of these women have the courage to keep going and looking for answers, to keep trying for the sometimes seemingly

If only pregnancy were as easy as a push of a button.

unattainable goal. You must remember that there is always hope. I have seen women who have tried for years to get pregnant. One in particular took eight years before she finally conceived. She went through IVF treatments, and in the end decided to go with a more holistic approach. She and her husband, in combination with a medical doctor and holistic practitioner, focused on balancing her energies and bringing her body back to center. She and her husband then created a ritual similar to the one below and they did indeed conceive.

If we look at fertility issues through the Psychic Sex Connection and therefore through the energy itself, it is like the negative and positive ends of batteries. If you are putting in a battery, the positive end must connect to it's counterpart, the negative. It is just a transference and completion of an energetic cycle. I look at fertility in the same way, if a man's energy is fragmented or skewed, then how is the energy to create a complete cycle? It simply cannot. We get so caught up in the stress that our bodies and minds put on us to have a child that sometimes we cannot even enjoy the act itself. Women are not like men, we do think during sex, I've heard many women complain at my table, "And when we are trying to make a baby, all

I keep thinking about is how badly I want it to work." It becomes a job, no longer a pleasure, but I have a solution.

Fertility rituals were rampant during the pagan times and I feel that they still have their place in the world today. I am not saying you need to become a witch, but the Psychic Sex Connection is like a ritual itself; it puts you into the mood and mindset of creating a link with your partner. Having a fertility ritual can do the same. Much of this is going to come from the woman's perspective, although it is very important that both potential parents be present so that the partner can lend their energies. In addition, you will notice that the focus is on a female deity. This is because in many cultures, when it comes to fertility, the Divine Feminine is often seen as the giver of life. Here is an example of one:

What you need:

A small bowl (in the shape of an apple)

A starfish

Soil from Mother Earth (not potting mix or store bought)

Milk (preferably, fresh and unprocessed but from a store is fine in a pinch)

A seed (of any kind)

Wooden Matches

A candle (pink if you would like a girl, light blue for a boy)

A bed or comfortable arrangement of pillows

Directions:

You want to be sure to conduct this ritual right around the time that the prospective mother is starting to ovulate, maybe even a few days in advance of the cycle. In this ritual you can pick your Goddess depending on your own belief system. I have listed just a few here.

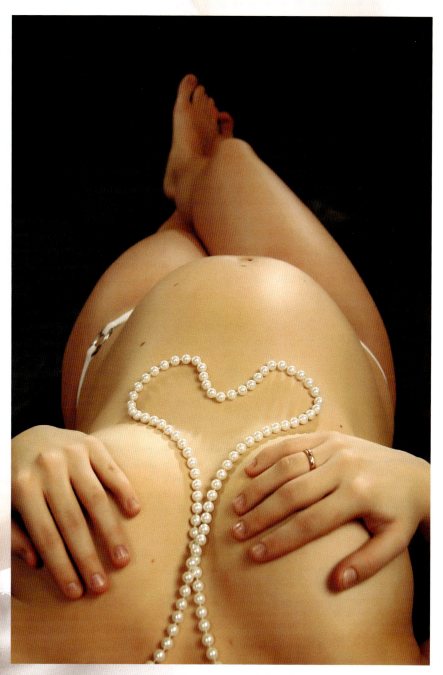

Pearls have long held connections to water and fertility. They are often used in rituals concerning pregnancy.

Celtic/Norse:
Freyja   Brigid   Hecate
Arianrhod   Macha

Greek/Roman:
Venus   Juno   Artemis

Egyptian:
Bastet   Hathor   Isis

Christian/Catholic Saints:
St. Anne   St. Catharine of Sweden
St. Monica   St. Margaret the Virgin

Once you have your Goddess or Saint in mind, I would suggest going on-line and getting a printout or buying a picture or statue of the Deity.

When you are ready to begin the ritual, you want to be protected—using the bubbling up technique as described earlier in the book will be fine. See it encompass the room in which you are about to do the ritual.

Invite your chosen Goddess or Saint to join you in your fertility ritual by saying something like:

_____ I ask you to join us _____ as we set forth our
(Goddess/Saint)   (today/tonight)

energies to creating a child. Aid us in our endeavors.

Gather your materials together and have the future mother put each of the items into it saying:

To the image of the sacred apple I add
A starfish from the waters of life
Soil from Mother Earth
Milk to symbolize the nectar of a mother's breast
A seed for growth, new life and fertility.

Light a match and touch each of the contents with it while saying:

> *A flame for the fire that burns within and the spark of creation.*

Place the pink/blue candle next to your bowl in a candle holder, have the mother light the candle while saying aloud:

> *I light the _____ candle to represent the _____ of my heart.*
>   (pink/blue)   (daughter/son)

Chant 3 times while you and your partner envision the baby:

> *_____, I ask of thee, Grant to us fertility*
> (Goddess/Saint)
>
> *Sperm join egg and blessed it be*
>
> *_____ babe to be born from me*
> (man's name)'s
>
> *With harm to none. New love to many. So mote it be*

Allow the candle to burn, gaze into the flame and visualize yourself holding your child in your arms as long as possible. If the candle goes out, the man should relight it. If not, allow it to continue burning on its own.

When you are ready, have the man take the apple bowl and matches in his hands. Proceed outside.

Both the man and woman should kneel in a private place on the property as the woman digs a small hole in the ground.

The man should then say aloud (as he places the contents of the apple into the hole):

> *_____ please join us here in this place*
> (Goddess/Saint)
> *From the image of the sacred apple,*
> *I place the following within Mother Earth:*
> *A starfish from the waters of life*
> *Soil returning to Mother Earth*
> *Milk to symbolize the nectar of a mother's breast - may it also feed the land*
> *A seed for growth, new life and fertility.*

He should then light a match and place it in the hole and then say:

A flame for the fire that burns within and the spark of creation

Within the cauldron burns the _____ candle
  (pink/blue)
to represent the _____ of my heart.
  (daughter/son)

_____ , I ask of thee. Grant to us fertility.
(Goddess/Saint)

Sperm join egg and blessed it be

_____ babe to be fathered by me
(woman's name)'s

With harm to none. New love to many. So mote it be.

The man should then replace the removed soil to refill the hole and say:

Thank you for your blessings _____ .
   (Goddess/Saint)

Return to your protective bubble, both of you again giving thanks to the Goddess.

Allow the candle to burn out. Lie down and make love.

The great thing about rituals like these is that you can modify them to your belief systems, change words and make them your own. One thing about ritual is mood. We talked about it earlier in the book and I am going to address it again here. Muted lighting is best, and when conducting rituals such as these, I often like to play music very lightly in the background. I prefer Egyptian music (depending on the artist) as the sounds often remind me of the old fertility rituals and belly dancing which once was a part of those ancient practices. The steady almost sensual beats help to create an atmosphere for loving, however, if you are more partial to Marvin Gaye, that's fine too. But I would suggest something that is more instrumental so as not to take away your focus.

ANOTHER one is a short little remedy specifically for the woman looking to have a child. However, men feel free to aid her—it can definitely make for a sensual evening.

What You Need:

Apple-scented body cream

String of pearls (faux pearls are fine)

Directions:

Perform this small ritual during your ovulation. Take a shower, cleansing every part of your body. You may want to even incorporate an apple-scented organic body wash. Get out of the shower and towel off. Using the apple scented lotion or body cream, massage it all over your body paying special attention to the belly (your hunny can help you at this point). Imagine that you and your partners hands are glowing with a golden brilliant light which fills your stomach and gives a feeling of warmth and life. Hold the pearls as you continue this visualization and now bring to the forefront a picture or "movie" of yourself pregnant, laughing, giggling ... as you do this, run the pearls through your hands and say:

Precious jewels of life giving water and the lunar moon,
I offer this adornment in honor of your power.
Let fertile light shine through me.

Chant this six times as you continue your visualization and run the pearls through your hands. Then go to your partner and make love.

There are also fertility oils that you can try which are both fun to make and use!

OKO Fertility Oil for Men

In 2oz vegetable base oil containing one capsule Vitamin E., mix:

    3 drops allspice

    2 drops ylang-ylang

    5 drops vanilla

Massage onto penis prior to having sex.

Yemaya Fertility Oil for Women

In 2oz vegetable base oil containing one capsule Vitamin E., mix:

    7 drops Watermelon

    3 drops Balsam

    1 drop Aster

Massage onto inner thighs or anoint yourself on pulse point's prior making love.

The whole point of these rituals and creations (aside from their spiritual properties) is to bring you focus and presence to the act of loving so that your stress level will go down. Granted, science has not found a link between stress and infertility ... yet, it certainly does not help to be stressed in any situation. So a proper focus combined with the energy that you are channeling into the Universe will help you in your fruitful endeavors.

In Conclusion

"If sex is such a natural phenomenon, how come there are so many books on how to do it?"

~*Bette Midler*

BETTE Midler asks a great question in the above quote. In answer, I think we write so much about sex because even though we understand the bio-mechanics, we do not understand the spirituality of sex. It has been drummed into us for so long that to enjoy sex is to be sinful, that to love sex is to be damned, that we are a society where each one of us is like a kid trying to steal a cookie. You know Mom will not let you have it. You know you may get in trouble for your ill behavior, but you become obsessed with the cookie. Sex is America's secret obsession, and everyone knows it but us.

I wrote this book to go beyond sex. Sex is merely the vehicle and you can apply many of the techniques I have written about in this book to your daily life (remember I said techniques, not positions). Sex is something that is transcendental, primal, and divine; it can be the worst enemy or pure bliss. I see so many of my clients who do not get enough alone time with their partner and if this can be a catalyst for you and your spouse, or significant other to reconnect, then my work here is done.

Follow your bliss, invoke the essence of Shiva and Shakti and reach new heights within yourself and your relationship. I wish you the best of happiness; the hottest of sex, and that you discover the Divinity that is you!

Brightest Blessings
Always,

Beckah Boyd

Resources

Beckah's Websites and Affiliations

http://beckahboydtarot.blogspot.com ~Beckah's weekly 'Tarotscopes'

http://www.beckahthepsychic.com ~The official Beckah Boyd website

http://www.ghostquest.org ~Beckah co-owns Ghost Quest Paranormal Society

http://www.mysteriesmagazine.com ~Beckah is the psychic advice columnist for *Mysteries Magazine*

http://www.tenacityradio.com ~Tenacity Radio is a station Beckah co-founded with Jeremiah Greer of *Mysteries Magazine* specializing in variety talk and music its great to listen to during the workday and at home!

http://www.thepsychicswitch.com ~Listen in to Beckah's radio show, *The Psychic Switch* discussing psychic phenomena in every capacity (including love) and be sure to sign up for the Generation Psychic Community

Photography and Graphic Design

http://www.capturedmomentsbykim.com ~Kimberly Taylor's website

http://www.bydesign.ws ~Shannon's Sylvia's Website

Stones and Herbs

Azuregreen/Abyss Distribution ~Stones, herbs, magical supplies. http://www.azuregreen.com

Crystal Herbs ~Great source for pure essential oils and Bach flower therapy oils. http://www.crystalherbs.com

Pelham Grayson ~Great seller of rough, tumbled, crystals, pendulums and more! Really good pricing too. http://www.pelhamgrayson.com

Products for Tantra

Body of The Goddess ~A wonderful website that sells everything from clothing to toys! Offering workshops on sacred sex and glorifying in the Goddess in you! http://www.bodyofthegoddess.com. (707) 543-6786

Tantra At Tahoe ~Official webpage of Jeffre and Somraj. Directors of the Academy of Supreme Bliss Tantra. http://www.tantraattahoe.com

Tantra World ~Chandi Devi's Website, a Goddess of Tantra her educational videos are great! http://www.theworldoftantra.com

The Tantra Chair ~It looks luxurious and classy, your friends will never know! http://www.tantrachair.com

Recommended Reading

Devi, Chandi. *From Om to Orgasm. The Tantra Primer for Living in Bliss.*

McGhee, Paul. *Health Healing and the Amuse System.* http://www.laughterremedy.com.

Scott-Mumby, Keith (Dr.). *Virtual Medicine.* ISBN 0722538235.

Stubbs, Kenneth Ray (Ph.D.). *Secret Sexual Positions.* Secret Garden Publishing. ISBN 9780939263158

Videos

Ehow.com ~ Richard Neil teaches you the art of Shiatsu Massage and the meridian lines. http://www.ehow.com/videos-on_3776_do-hara-leg-shiatsu-massages.html

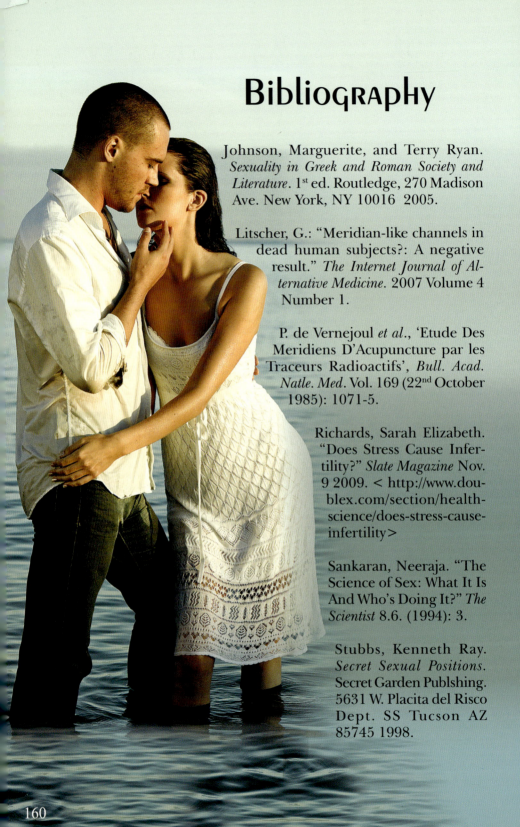

Bibliography

Johnson, Marguerite, and Terry Ryan. *Sexuality in Greek and Roman Society and Literature*. 1st ed. Routledge, 270 Madison Ave. New York, NY 10016 2005.

Litscher, G.: "Meridian-like channels in dead human subjects?: A negative result." *The Internet Journal of Alternative Medicine*. 2007 Volume 4 Number 1.

P. de Vernejoul *et al.*, 'Etude Des Meridiens D'Acupuncture par les Traceurs Radioactifs', *Bull. Acad. Natle. Med.* Vol. 169 (22nd October 1985): 1071-5.

Richards, Sarah Elizabeth. "Does Stress Cause Infertility?" *Slate Magazine* Nov. 9 2009. < http://www.doublex.com/section/health-science/does-stress-cause-infertility>

Sankaran, Neeraja. "The Science of Sex: What It Is And Who's Doing It?" *The Scientist* 8.6. (1994): 3.

Stubbs, Kenneth Ray. *Secret Sexual Positions*. Secret Garden Publshing. 5631 W. Placita del Risco Dept. SS Tucson AZ 85745 1998.